RCMP Police Aptitude (RPAT) Study Guide & Practice Test Questions

Published by

Complete TEST™ Preparation Inc.

Copyright © 2015 by Complete Test Preparation Inc. ALL RIGHTS RESERVED. No part of this book may be reproduced or transferred in any form or by any means, graphic, electronic, or mechanical, including photocopying, recording, web distribution, taping, or by any information storage retrieval system, without the written permission of the author.

Notice: Complete Test Preparation Inc. makes every reasonable effort to obtain from reliable sources accurate, complete, and timely information about the tests covered in this book. Nevertheless, changes can be made in the tests or the administration of the tests at any time and Complete Test Preparation Inc. makes no representation or warranty, either expressed or implied as to the accuracy, timeliness, or completeness of the information contained in this book. Complete Test Preparation Inc. makes no representations or warranties of any kind, express or implied, about the completeness, accuracy, reliability, suitability or availability with respect to the information contained in this document for any purpose. Any reliance you place on such information is therefore strictly at your own risk.

The author(s) shall not be liable for any loss incurred as a consequence of the use and application, directly or indirectly, of any information presented in this work. Sold with the understanding, the author(s) is not engaged in rendering professional services or advice. If advice or expert assistance is required, the services of a competent professional should be sought.

The company, product and service names used in this publication are for identification purposes only. All trademarks and registered trademarks are the property of their respective owners. Complete Test Preparation Inc. is not affiliated with any educational institution.

Complete Test Preparation Inc. is not affiliated with any RCMP Service, who are not involved in the production of, and do not endorse this publication.

We strongly recommend that students check with exam providers for up-to-date information regarding test content.

Published by
Complete Test Preparation Inc.
Victoria BC Canada
Visit us on the web at http://www.test-preparation.ca
Printed in the USA

About Complete Test Preparation Inc.

Complete Test Preparation Inc. has been publishing high quality study materials since 2005. Thousands of students visit our websites every year, and thousands of students, teachers and parents all over the world have purchased our teaching materials, curriculum, study guides and practice tests.

Complete Test Preparation Inc. is committed to providing students with the best study materials and practice tests available on the market. Members of our team combine years of teaching experience, with experienced writers and editors, all with advanced degrees.

ISBN-13: 9781928077077

Version 7.3 February 2017

Feedback

We welcome your feedback. Email us at feedback@test-preparation.ca with your comments and suggestions. We carefully review all suggestions and often incorporate reader suggestions into upcoming versions. As a Print on Demand Publisher, we update our products frequently.

Find us on Facebook

www.facebook.com/CompleteTestPreparation

Contents

Getting Started

CONGRATULATIONS! By deciding to take the RCMP Police Aptitude Test, you have taken the first step toward a great future! Of course, there is no point in taking this important examination unless you intend to do your best to earn the highest grade you possibly can. That means getting yourself organized and discovering the best approaches, methods and strategies to master the material. Yes, that will require real effort and dedication on your part, but if you are willing to focus your energy and devote the study time necessary, before you know it you will be on you way to a brighter future!

We know that taking on a new endeavour can be scary, and it is easy to feel unsure of where to begin. That's where we come in. This study guide is designed to help you improve your test-taking skills, show you a few tricks of the trade and increase both your competency and confidence.

The RCMP Police Aptitude Test

The RCMP is composed of six sections,

Observation – This section tests your ability to remember details

- **Reading Comprehension**
- **Composition** – This section tests your ability to articulate in writing, complex thoughts in a clear and concise way that is understandable to others. This includes, vocabulary, spelling and English grammar.

- **Professional Judgement**
- **Recognition/Identification** – Here you are shown a face and asked to choose the same person from four pictures, where their appearance has been altered.
- **Logic** – This section tests your ability to analyze situations. Questions include, ordering pieces of information into a logical sequence, reading a map, identifying patterns in data, and solving problems
- **Simple Word Problems** (Basic Math)

While we seek to make our guide as comprehensive as possible, note that like all exams, the RCMP Exam might be adjusted at some future point. New material might be added, or content that is no longer relevant or applicable might be removed. It is always a good idea to give the materials you receive when you register to take the RCMP test a careful review.

How this study guide is organized

This study guide is divided into three sections. The first section, Self-Assessments, will help you recognize your areas of strength and weakness. This will be a boon when it comes to managing your study time most efficiently; there is not much point of focusing on material you have already got firmly under control. Instead, taking the self-assessments will show you where that time could be much better spent. In this area you will begin with a few questions to evaluate quickly your understanding of material that is likely to appear on the RCMP test. If you do poorly in certain areas, simply work carefully through those sections in the tutorials and then try the self-assessment again.

The second section, Tutorials, offers information in each of the content areas, as well as strategies to help you master that material. The tutorials are not intended to be a complete course, but cover general principles. If you find that you do not understand the tutorials, it is recommended that you seek out additional instruction.

Third, we offer two sets of practice test questions, similar to those on the RCMP Exam.

The RCMP Study Plan

Now that you have made the decision to take the RCMP test, it is time to get started. Before you do another thing, you will need to figure out a plan of attack. The very best study tip is to start early! The longer the time period you devote to regular study practice, the more likely you will be to retain the material and be able to access it quickly. If you thought that 1x20 is the same as 2x10, guess what? It really is not, when it comes to study time. Reviewing material for just an hour per day over the course of 20 days is far better than studying for two hours a day for only 10 days. The more often you revisit a particular piece of information, the better you will know it. Not only will your grasp and understanding be better, but your ability to reach into your brain and quickly and efficiently pull out the tidbit you need, will be greatly enhanced as well.

The great Chinese scholar and philosopher Confucius believed that true knowledge could be defined as knowing both what you know and what you do not know. The first step in preparing for the RCMP is to assess your strengths and weaknesses. You may already have an idea of what you know and what you do not know, but evaluating yourself using our Self- Assessment modules for each of the test content areas may surprise you.

Making a Study Schedule

To make your study time the most productive you will need to develop a study plan. The purpose of the plan is to organize all the bits of pieces of information in such a way that you will not feel overwhelmed. Rome was not built in a day, and learning everything you will need to know to pass the RCMP is going to take time, too. Arranging the material you need to learn into manageable chunks is the best way to go. Each study session should make you feel as though you have succeeded in accomplishing your goal, and your goal is simply to learn what you planned to learn during that particular session. Try to organize the content in such a way that each study session builds on previous ones. That way, you will retain the information, be better able to access it, and review the previous bits and pieces at the same time.

Self-assessment

The Best Study Tip! The very best study tip is to start early! The longer you study regularly, the more you will retain and 'learn' the material. Studying for 1 hour per day for 20 days is far better than studying for 2 hours for 10 days.

What don't you know?

The first step is to assess your strengths and weaknesses. You may already have an idea of where your weaknesses are, or you can take our Self-assessment modules for each of the content areas.

Exam Component	**Rate 1 to 5**
Reading Comprehension	
Composition	
Vocabulary	
Spelling	

English Grammar	
Professional Judgement	
Recognition/Identification	
Logic	
Ordering information	
Identifying sequences	
Solving Problems	
Basic Math	
Percent	
Decimals	
Word Problems	

Making a Study Schedule

The key to making a study plan is to divide the material you need to learn into manageable sized pieces and learn it, while at the same time reviewing the material that you already know.

Using the table above, any scores of 3 or below, you need to spend time learning, reviewing and practicing this subject area. A score of 4 means you need to review the material, but you don't have to spend time re-learning. A score of 5 and you are OK with just an occasional review before the exam.

A score of 0 or 1 means you really need to work on this should allocate the most time and the highest priority. Some students prefer a 5-day plan and others a 10-day plan. It also depends on how much time you have until the exam.

Here is an example of a 5-day plan based on an example from the table above:

Reading Comprehension: 1- Study 1 hour everyday – review on last day
Vocabulary: 3 - Study 1 hour for 3 days then ½ hour a day, then review
Word Problems: 4 - Review every second day
Professional Judgement: 5 - Review for ½ hour every other day
Logic: 5 - Review for ½ hour every other day

Using this example, logic and professional judgement are good, and only need occasional review. Vocabulary is good and needs 'some' review. Reading Comprehension is very weak and need most of your time. Based on this, here is a sample study plan:

Day	Subject	Time
Monday		
Study	Reading Comprehension	1 hour
Study	Word Problems	1 hour
½ hour break		
Study	Vocabulary	1 hour
Review	Reading Comp.	½ hour
Tuesday		
Study	Reading Comprehension	1 hour
Study	Word Problems	½ hour
½ hour break		
Study	Vocabulary	½ hour
Review	Professional Judgement	½ hour
Review	Logic	½ hour
Wednesday		
Study	Reading Comprehension	1 hour
Study	Word Problems	½ hour
½ hour break		
Study	Vocabulary	½ hour
Review	Reading Comp.	½ hour
Thursday		
Study	Reading Comprehension	½ hour
Study	Word Problems	½ hour
Review	Vocabulary	½ hour
½ hour break		
Review	Logic	½ hour
Review	Professional Judgement	½ hour
Friday		
Review	Reading Comprehension	½ hour
Review	Word Problems	½ hour
Review	Vocabulary	½ hour
½ hour break		
Review	Professional Judgement	½ hour
Review	Logic	½ hour

Using this example, adapt the study plan to your own schedule. This schedule assumes 2 ½ - 3 hours available to study everyday for a 5 day period.

First, write out what you need to study and how much. Next figure out how many days before the test. Note, do NOT study on the last day before the test. On the last day before the test, you won't learn anything and will probably only confuse yourself.

Make a table with the days before the test and the number of hours you have available to study each day. We suggest working with 1 hour and ½ hour time slots.

Start filling in the blanks, with the subjects you need to study the most getting the most time and the most regular time slots (i.e. everyday) and the subjects that you know getting the least time (e.g. ½ hour every other day, or every 3rd day).

Tips for making a schedule

Once you make a schedule, stick with it! Make your study sessions reasonable. If you make a study schedule and don't stick with it, you set yourself up for failure. Instead, schedule study sessions that are a bit shorter and set yourself up for success! Make sure your study sessions are do-able. Studying is hard work but after you pass, you can party and take a break!

Schedule breaks. Breaks are just as important as study time. Work out a rotation of studying and breaks that works for you.

Build up study time. If you find it hard to sit still and study for 1 hour straight through, build up to it. Start with 20 minutes, and then take a break. Once you get used to 20-minute study sessions, increase the time to 30 minutes. Gradually work you way up to 1 hour.

40 minutes to 1 hour is optimal. Studying for longer than this is tiring and not productive. Studying for shorter isn't long enough to be productive.

Studying Math. Studying Math is different from studying other subjects because you use a different part of your brain. The best way to study math is to practice everyday. This will train your mind to think in a mathematical way. If you miss a day or days, the mathematical mind-set is gone, and you have to start all over again to build it up.

Study and practice math everyday for at least 5 days before the exam.

For additional information on getting organized to study, see our How to Study book at www.study-skills.ca.

Reading Comprehension

THIS SECTION CONTAINS A SELF-ASSESSMENT AND READING TUTORIAL. The tutorials are designed to familiarize general principles and the self-assessment contains general questions similar to the reading questions likely to be on the RCMP exam, but are not intended to be identical to the exam questions. The tutorials are not designed to be a complete reading course, and it is assumed that students have some familiarity with reading comprehension and vocabulary questions. If you do not understand parts of the tutorial, or find the tutorial difficult, it is recommended that you seek out additional instruction.

For addition practice and help with reading comprehension see our Multiple Choice Secrets books at www.multiple-choice.ca.

Tour of the Reading Content

Below is a detailed list of the types of reading questions that generally appear on your exam.

- Drawing logical conclusions
- Make predictions
- Analyze and evaluate the use of text structure to solve problems or identify sequences
- Vocabulary - Give the definition of a word from context
- Summarize

The questions below are not the same as you will find on the exam - that would be too easy! And nobody knows what the questions will be and they change all the time. Mostly the changes consist of substituting new questions for old, but the changes can be new question formats or styles, changes to the number of questions in each section, changes to the time limits for each section and combining sections. Below are general reading and vocabulary questions that cover the same areas as the exam. So the format and exact wording of the questions may differ slightly, and change from year to year, if you can answer the questions below, you will have no problem with the reading section.

Reading Comprehension Self-Assessment

The purpose of the self-assessment is:

- Identify your strengths and weaknesses.
- Develop your personalized study plan (above)
- Get accustomed to the RCMP test format
- Extra practice – the self-assessments are almost a full 3rd practice test!
- Provide a baseline score for preparing your study schedule.

Since this is a self-assessment, and depending on how confident you are with reading comprehension and vocabulary, timing is optional. This self-assessment has 34 questions, so allow about 20 minutes to complete this assessment.

Once complete, use the table below to assess your understanding of the content, and prepare your study schedule described in chapter 1.

Questions 1 – 4 refer to the following passage.

The Immune System

An immune system is a system of biological structures and processes that protects against disease by identifying and killing pathogens and other threats. The immune system can detect a wide variety of agents, from viruses to parasitic worms, and distinguish them from the organism's own healthy cells and tissues. Detection is complicated as pathogens evolve rapidly to avoid the immune system defences, and successfully infect their hosts.

The human immune system consists of many types of proteins, cells, organs, and tissues, which interact in an elaborate and dynamic network. As part of this more complex immune response, the human immune system adapts over time to recognize specific pathogens more efficiently. This adaptation process is called "adaptive immunity" or "acquired immunity" and creates immunological memory. Immunological memory created from a primary response to a specific pathogen, provides an enhanced response to future encounters with that same pathogen. This process of acquired immunity is the basis of vaccination. [1]

1. What can we infer from the first paragraph in this passage?

a. When a person's body fights off the flu, this is the immune system in action

b. When a person's immune system functions correctly, they avoid all sicknesses and injuries

c. When a person's immune system is weak, a person will likely get a terminal disease

d. When a person's body fights off a cold, this is the circulatory system in action

2. The immune system's primary function is to:

a. Strengthen the bones

b. Protect against disease

c. Improve respiration

d. Improve circulation

3. Based on the passage, what can we say about evolution's role in the immune system?

a. Evolution of the immune system is an important factor in the immune system's efficiency

b. Evolution causes a person to die, thus killing the pathogen

c. Evolution plays no known role in immunity

d. The least evolved earth species have better immunity

4. Which sentence below, taken from the passage, tell us the main idea of the passage?

a. The human immune system consists of many types of proteins, cells, organs, and tissues, which interact in an elaborate and dynamic network.

b. An immune system is a system of biological structures and processes that protects against disease by identifying and killing pathogens and other threats.

c. The immune system can detect a wide variety of agents, from viruses to parasitic worms, and distinguish them from the organism's own healthy cells and tissues.

d. None of these express the main idea.

Questions 5 – 8 refer to the following passage.

White Blood Cells

White blood cells (WBCs), or leukocytes (also spelled "leucocytes"), are cells of the immune system that defend the body against both infectious disease and foreign material. Five different and diverse types of leukocytes exist, but they are all produced and derived from a powerful cell in the bone marrow known as a hematopoietic stem cell. Leukocytes are found throughout the body, including the blood and lymphatic system.

The number of WBCs in the blood is often an indicator of disease. There are normally between 4×10^9 and 1.1×10^{10} white blood cells in a liter of blood, making up about 1% of blood in a healthy adult. The physical properties of white blood cells, such as volume, conductivity, and granularity, changes due to the presence of immature cells, or malignant cells.

The name white blood cell derives from the fact that after processing a blood sample in a centrifuge, the white cells are typically a thin, white layer of nucleated cells. The scientific term leukocyte directly reflects this description, derived from Greek leukos (white), and kytos (cell). [2]

5. What can we infer from the first paragraph in this selection?

a. Red blood cells are not as important as white blood cells

b. White blood cells are the culprits in most infectious diseases

c. White blood cells are essential to fight off infectious diseases

d. Red blood cells are essential to fight off infectious diseases

6. What can we say about the number of white blood cells in a liter of blood?

a. They make up about 1% of a healthy adult's blood

b. There are 10^{10} WBCs in a healthy adult's blood

c. The number varies according to age

d. They are a thin white layer of nucleated cells

7. What is a more scientific term for "white blood cell?"

a. Red blood cell

b. Anthrocyte

c. Leukocyte

d. Leukemia

8. Can the number of leukocytes indicate cancer?

a. Yes, the white blood cell count can indicate disease.

b. No, the white blood cell count is not a reliable indicator.

c. Disease may indicate a high white blood cell count.

d. None of the choices are correct.

Questions 9 – 12 refer to the following passage.

Keeping Tropical Fish

Keeping tropical fish at home or in your office used to be very popular. Today interest has declined, but it remains as rewarding and relaxing a hobby as ever. Ask any tropical fish hobbyist, and you will hear how soothing and relaxing watching colorful fish live their lives in the aquarium. If you are considering keeping tropical fish as pets, here is a list of the basic equipment you will need.

A filter is essential for keeping your aquarium clean and your fish alive and healthy. There are different types and sizes of filters and the right size for you depends on the size of the aquarium and the level of stocking. Generally, you need a filter with a 3 to 5 times turn over rate per hour. This means that the water in the tank should go through the filter about 3 to 5 times per hour.

Most tropical fish do well in water temperatures ranging between 24^0 C and 26^0 C, though each has its own ideal water temperature. A heater with a thermostat is necessary to regulate the water temperature. Some heaters are submersible and others are not, so check carefully before you buy.

Lights are also necessary, and come in a large variety of types, strengths and sizes. A light source is necessary for plants in the tank to photosynthesize and give the tank a more attractive appearance. Even if you plan to use plastic plants, the fish still require light, although here, you can use a lower strength light source.

A hood is necessary to keep dust, dirt and unwanted materials out of the tank. Sometimes the hood can also help prevent evaporation. Another requirement is aquarium gravel. This will help improve the aesthetics of the aquarium and is necessary if you plan to have real plants.

9. What is the general tone of this article?

a. Formal

b. Informal

c. Technical

d. Opinion

10. Which of the following cannot be inferred?

a. Gravel is good for aquarium plants.

b. Fewer people have aquariums in their office than at home.

c. The larger the tank, the larger the filter required.

d. None of the above.

11. What evidence does the author provide to support their claim that aquarium lights are necessary?

a. Plants require light.

b. Fish and plants require light.

c. The author does not provide evidence for this statement.

d. Aquarium lights make the aquarium more attractive.

12. Which of the following is an opinion?

a. Filter with a 3 to 5 times turn over rate per hour are required.

b. Aquarium gravel improves the aesthetics of the aquarium.

c. An aquarium hood keeps dust, dirt and unwanted materials out of the tank.

d. Each type of tropical fish has its own ideal water temperature.

Questions 13 – 14 refer to the following passage.

Vice President Johnson, Mr. Speaker, Mr. Chief Justice, President Eisenhower, Vice President Nixon, President Truman, reverend clergy, fellow citizens:

We observe today not a victory of party, but a celebration of freedom -- symbolizing an end, as well as a beginning -- signifying renewal, as well as change. For I have sworn before you and Almighty God the same solemn oath our forebears prescribed nearly a century and three-quarters ago.

The world is very different now. For man holds in his mortal hands the power to abolish all forms of human poverty and all forms of human life. And yet the same revolutionary beliefs for which our forebears fought are still at issue around the globe -- the belief that the rights of man come not from the generosity of the state, but from the hand of God.

We dare not forget today that we are the heirs of that first revolution. Let the word go forth from this time and place, to friend and foe alike, that the torch has been passed to a new generation of Americans -- born in this century, tempered by war, disciplined by a hard and bitter peace, proud of our ancient heritage, and unwilling to witness or permit the slow undoing of those human rights to which this nation has always been committed, and to which we are committed today at home and around the world.

Let every nation know, whether it wishes us well or ill, that we shall pay any price, bear any burden, meet any hardship, support any friend, oppose any foe, to assure the survival and the success of liberty.

This much we pledge -- and more.

John F. Kennedy Inaugural Address 20 January 1961

13. What is the tone of this speech?

a. Triumphant
b. Optimistic
c. Threatening
d. Gloating

14. Which of the following is an opinion?

a. The world is very different now.

b. For man holds in his mortal hands the power to abolish all forms of human poverty and all forms of human life.

c. We dare not forget today that we are the heirs of that first revolution

d. For I have sworn before you and Almighty God the same solemn oath our forebears prescribed nearly a century and three-quarters ago.

Reading Self-Assessment Answer Key

1. A
The passage does not mention the flu specifically, however we know the flu is a pathogen (a bacterium, virus, or other microorganism that can cause disease). Therefore, we can infer, when a person's body fights off the flu, this is the immune system in action.

2. B
The immune system's primary function is to protect against disease.

3. A
The passage refers to evolution of the immune system being important for efficiency. In paragraph three, there is a discussion of adaptive and acquired immunity, where the immune system "remembers" pathogens.

We can conclude, evolution of the immune system is an important factor in the immune system's efficiency.

4. B
The sentence that expresses the main idea of the passage is, "An immune system is a system of biological structures and processes that protects against disease by identifying and killing pathogens and other threats."

5. C
We can infer white blood cells are essential to fight off infectious diseases, from the passage, "cells of the immune system that defend the body against both infectious disease and foreign material."

6. A
We can say the number of white blood cells in a liter of blood make up about 1% of a healthy adult's blood. This is a fact-based question that is easy and fast to answer. The question asks about a percentage. You can quickly and easily scan the passage for the percent sign, or the word percent and find the answer.

7. C
A more scientific term for "white blood cell" is leukocyte, from the first paragraph, first sentence of the passage.

8. A
The white blood cell count can indicate disease (cancer). We know this from the last sentence of paragraph two, "The physical properties of white blood cells, such as volume, conductivity, and granularity, changes due to the presence of immature cells, or malignant cells."

9. B
The general tone is informal.

10. B
The statement, "Fewer people have aquariums in their office than at home," cannot be inferred from this article.

11. C
The author does not provide evidence for this statement.

12. B
The following statement is an opinion, "Aquarium gravel improves the aesthetics of the aquarium."

13. A
This is a triumphant speech where President Kennedy is celebrating his victory.

14. C
The statement, "We dare not forget today that we are the heirs of that first revolution" is an opinion.

Help with Reading Comprehension

At first sight, reading comprehension tests look challenging especially if you are given long essays to answer only two to three questions. While reading, you might notice your attention wandering, or you may feel sleepy. Do not be discouraged because there are various tactics and long range strategies that make comprehending even long, boring essays easier.

Your friends before your foes. It is always best to tackle essays or passages with familiar subjects rather than those with unfamiliar ones. This approach applies the same logic as tackling easy questions before hard ones. Skip passages that do not interest you and leave them for later when there is more time.

Don't use 'special' reading techniques. This is not the time for speed-reading or anything like that – just plain ordinary reading – not too slow and not too fast.

Read through the entire passage and the questions before you do anything. Many students try reading the questions first and then looking for answers in the passage thinking this approach is more efficient. What these students do not realize is that it is often hard to navigate in unfamiliar roads. If you do not familiarize yourself with the passage first, looking for answers become not only time-consuming but also dangerous because you might miss the context of the answer you are looking for. If you read the questions first you will only confuse yourself and lose valuable time.

Familiarize yourself with reading comprehension questions. If you are familiar with the common types of reading questions, you are able to take note of important parts of the passage, saving time. There are six major kinds of reading questions.

- **Main Idea**- Questions that ask for the central thought or significance of the passage.

- **Specific Details** - Questions that asks for explicitly stated ideas.

- **Drawing Inferences** - Questions that ask for a statement's intended meaning.

- **Tone or Attitude** - Questions that test your ability to sense the emotional state of the author.

- **Context Meaning** – Questions that ask for the meaning of a word depending on the context.

- **Technique** – Questions that ask for the method of organization or the writing style of the author.

Read. Read. Read. The best preparation for reading comprehension tests is always to read, read and read. If you are not used to reading lengthy passages, you will probably lose concentration. Increase your attention span by making a habit out of reading.

Reading Comprehension tests become less daunting when you have trained yourself to read and understand fast. Always remember that it is easier to understand passages you are interested in. Do not read through passages hastily. Make mental notes of ideas that you think might be asked.

Reading Strategy

When facing the reading comprehension section of a standardized test, you need a strategy to be successful. You want to keep several steps in mind:

- **First, make a note of the time and the number of sections.** Time your work accordingly. Typically, four to five minutes per section is sufficient. Second, read the directions for each selection thoroughly before beginning (and listen well to any additional verbal instructions, as they will often clarify obscure or confusing written guidelines). You must know exactly how to do what you're about to do!

• **Now you're ready to begin reading the selection.** Read the passage carefully, noting significant characters or events on a scratch sheet of paper or underlining on the test sheet. Many students find making a basic list in the margins helpful. Quickly jot down or underline one-word summaries of characters, notable happenings, numbers, or key ideas. This will help you better retain information and focus wandering thoughts. Remember, however, that your main goal in doing this is to find the information that answers the questions. Even if you find the passage interesting, remember your goal and work fast but stay on track.

• Now read the question and all of the choices. Now you have read the passage, have a general idea of the main ideas, and have marked the important points. Read the question and all of the choices. Never choose an answer without reading them all! Questions are often designed to confuse – stay focussed and clear. Usually the answer choices will focus on one or two facts or inferences from the passage. Keep these clear in your mind.

• **Search for the answer.** With a very general idea of what the different choices are, go back to the passage and scan for the relevant information. Watch for big words, unusual or unique words. These make your job easier as you can scan the text for the particular word.

• Mark the Answer. Now you have the key information the question is looking for. Go back to the question, quickly scan the choices and mark the correct one.

Understand and practice the different types of standardized reading comprehension tests. See the list above for the different types. Typically, there will be several questions dealing with facts from the selection, a couple more inference questions dealing with logical consequences of those facts, and periodically an application-oriented question surfaces to force you to make connections with what you already know. Some students prefer to answer the questions as listed, and feel classifying the question and then ordering is wasting precious time. Other students prefer to answer the different types of questions in order of how easy or difficult they are. The choice is yours and do whatever works for you. If you want to try answering in order of difficulty, here is a recommended order, answer fact questions first; they're easily found within the passage. Tackle inference problems next, after re-reading the question(s) as many times as you need to. Application or 'best guess' questions usually take the longest, so save them for last.

Use the practice tests to try out both ways of answering and see what works for you.

For more help with reading comprehension, see Multiple Choice Secrets at www,multiple-choice.ca

Main Idea and Supporting Details

Identifying the main idea, topic and supporting details in a passage can feel like an overwhelming task. The passages used for standardized tests can be boring and seem difficult - Test writers don't use interesting passages or ones that talk about things most people are familiar with. Despite these obstacles, all passages and paragraphs will have the information you need to answer the questions.

The topic of a passage or paragraph is its subject. It's the general idea and can be summed up in a word or short phrase. On some standardized tests, there is a short description of the passage if it's taken from a longer work. Make sure you read the description as it might state the topic of the passage. If not, read the passage and ask yourself, "Who or what is this about?" For example:

> Over the years, school uniforms have been hotly debated. Arguments are made that students have the right to show individuality and express themselves by choosing their own clothes. However, this brings up social and academic issues. Some kids cannot afford to wear the clothes they like and might be bullied by the "better dressed" students. With attention drawn to clothes and the individual, students will lose focus on class work and the reason they are in school. School uniforms should be mandatory.

Ask: What is this paragraph about?

Topic: school uniforms

Once you have the topic, it's easier to find the main idea. The main idea is a specific statement telling what the writer wants you to know about the topic. Writers usually state the main idea as a thesis statement. If you're looking for the main idea of a single paragraph, the main idea is called the topic sentence and will probably be the first or last sentence. If you're looking for the main idea of an entire passage, look for the thesis statement in either the first or last paragraph. The main idea is usually restated in the conclusion. To find the main idea of a passage or paragraph, follow these steps:

1. Find the topic.

2. Ask yourself, "What point is the author trying to make about the topic?"

3. Create your own sentence summarizing the author's point.

4. Look in the text for the sentence closest in meaning to yours.

Look at the example paragraph again. It's already established that the topic of the paragraph is school uniforms. What is the main idea/topic sentence?

Ask: "What point is the author trying to make about school uniforms?"

Summary: Students should wear school uniforms.

Topic sentence: School uniforms should be mandatory.

Main Idea: School uniforms should be mandatory.

Each paragraph offers supporting details to explain the main idea. The details could be facts or reasons, but they will always answer a question about the main idea. What? Where? Why? When? How? How much/many? Look at the example paragraph again. You'll notice that more than one sentence answers a question about the main idea. These are the supporting details.

Main Idea: School uniforms should be mandatory.

Ask: Why? Some kids cannot afford to wear clothes they like and could be bullied by the "better dressed" kids. Supporting Detail

With attention drawn to clothes and the individual, Students will lose focus on class work and the reason they are in school (Supporting Detail).

What if the author doesn't state the main idea in a topic sentence? The passage will have an implied main idea. It's not as difficult to find as it might seem. Paragraphs are always organized around ideas. To find an implied main idea, you need to know the topic and then find the relationship between the supporting details. Ask yourself, "What is the point the author is making about the relationship between the details?"

> Cocoa is what makes chocolate good for you. Chocolate comes in many varieties. These delectable flavors include milk chocolate, dark chocolate, semi-sweet, and white chocolate.

Ask: What is this paragraph about?

Topic: Chocolate

Ask: What? Where? Why? When? How? How much/many?

Supporting details: Chocolate is good for you because it is made of cocoa, Chocolate is delicious, Chocolate comes in different delicious flavors

Ask: What is the relationship between the details and what is the author's point?

Main Idea: Chocolate is good because it is healthy and it tastes good.

Testing Tips for Main Idea Questions

1. Skim the questions – not the answer choices - before reading the passage.

2. Questions about main idea might use the words "theme," "generalization," or "purpose."

3. Save questions about the main idea for last. On standardized tests like the SAT, the answers to the rest of the questions can be found in order in the passage.

3. Underline topic sentences in the passage. Most tests allow you to write in your testing booklet.

4. Answer the question in your own words before looking at the answer choices. Then match your answer with an answer choice.

5. Cross out incorrect answer choices immediately to prevent confusion.

6. If two of the answer choices mean the same thing but use different words, they are BOTH incorrect.

7. If a question asks about the whole passage, cross out the answer choices that apply only to part of it.

8. If only part of the information is correct, that answer choice is incorrect.

9. An answer choice that is too broad is incorrect. All information needs to be backed up by the passage.

10. Answer choices with extreme wording are usually incorrect.

Drawing Inferences And Conclusions

Drawing inferences and making conclusions happens all the time. In fact, you probably do it every time you read—sometimes without even realizing it! For example, remember the first time you saw the movie "The Lion King." When you meet Scar for the first time, he is trapping a helpless mouse with his sharp claws preparing to eat it. When you see this action you guess that Scar is going to be a bad character in the movie. Nothing appeared to tell you this. No caption came across the bottom of the screen that said "Bad Guy." No red arrow pointed to Scar and said "Evil Lion." No, you made an inference about his character based on the context clue you were given. You do the same thing when you read!

When you draw an inference or make a conclusion you are doing the same thing, you are making an educated guess based on the hints the author gives you. We call these hints "context clues." Scar trapping the innocent mouse is the context clue about Scar's character.

Usually you are making inferences and drawing conclusions the entire time that you are reading. Whether you realize it or not, you are constantly making educated guesses based on context clues. Think about a time you were reading a book and something happened that you were expecting to happen. You're not psychic! Actually, you were picking up on the context clues and making inferences about what was going to happen next!

Let's try an easy example. Read the following sentences and answer the questions at the end of the passage.

Shelly really likes to help people. She loves her job because she gets to help people every single day. However, Shelly has to work long hours and she can get called in the middle of the night for emergencies. She wears a white lab coat at work and usually she carries a stethoscope.

What is most likely Shelly's job?

a. Musician
b. Lawyer
c. Doctor
d. Teacher

This probably seemed easy. Drawing inferences isn't always this simple, but it is the same basic principle. How did you know Shelly was a doctor? She helps people, she works long hours, she wears a white lab coat, and she gets called in for emergencies at night. Context Clues! Nowhere in the paragraph did it say Shelly was a doctor, but you were able to draw that conclusion based on the information provided in the paragraph. This is how it's done!

There is a catch, though. Remember that when you draw inferences based on reading, you should only use the information given to you by the author. Sometimes it is easy for us to make conclusions based on knowledge that is already in our mind—but that can lead you to drawing an incorrect inference. For example, let's pretend there is a bully at your school named Brent. Now let's say you read a story and the main character's name is Brent. You could NOT infer that the character in the story is a bully just because his name is Brent. You should only use the information given to you by the author to avoid drawing the wrong conclusion.

Let's try another example. Read the passage below and answer the question.

Social media is an extremely popular new form of connecting and communicating over the internet. Since Facebook's original launch in 2004, millions of people have joined in the social media craze. In fact, it is estimated that almost 75% of all internet users aged 18 and older use some form of social media. Facebook started at Harvard University as a way to get students connected. However, it quickly grew into a worldwide phenomenon and today, the founder of Facebook, Mark Zuckerberg has an estimated net worth of 28.5 billion dollars.

Facebook is not the only social media platform, though. Other sites such as Twitter, Instagram, and Snapchat have since been invented and are quickly becoming just as popular! Many social media users actually use more than one type of social media. Furthermore, most social media sites have created mobile apps that allow people to connect via social media virtually anywhere in the world!

What is the most likely reason that other social media sites like Twitter and Instagram were created?

a. Professors at Harvard University made it a class project.

b. Facebook was extremely popular and other people thought they could also be successful by designing social media sites.

c. Facebook was not connecting enough people.

d. Mark Zuckerberg paid people to invent new social media sites because he wanted lots of competition.

Here, the correct answer is B. Facebook was extremely popular and other people thought they could also be successful by designing social media sites. How do we know this? What are the context clues? Take a look at the first paragraph. What do we know based on this paragraph? Well, one sentence refers to Facebook's original launch. This suggests that Facebook was one of the first social media sites. In addition, we know that the founder of Facebook has been extremely successful and is worth billions of dollars. From this we can infer that other people wanted to imitate Facebook's idea and become just as successful as Mark Zuckerberg.

Let's go through the other answers. If you chose A, it might be because Facebook started at Harvard University, so you drew the conclusion that all other social media sites were also started at Harvard University. However, there is no mention of class projects, professors, or students designing social media. So there doesn't seem to be enough support for choice A.

If you chose C, you might have been drawing your own conclusions based on outside information. Maybe none of your friends are on Facebook, so you made an inference that Facebook didn't connect enough people, so more sites were invented. Or maybe you think the people who connect on Facebook are too old, so you don't think Facebook connects enough people your age. This might be true, but remember inferences should be drawn from the information the author gives you!

If you chose D, you might be using the information that Mark Zuckerberg is worth over 28 billion dollars. It would be easy for him to pay others to design new sites, but remember, you need to use context clues! He is very wealthy, but that statement was giving you information about how successful Facebook was—not suggesting that he paid others to design more sites!

So remember, drawing inferences and conclusions is simply about using the information you are given to make an educated guess. You do this every single day so don't let this concept scare you. Look for the context clues, make sure they support your claim, and you'll be able to make accurate inferences and conclusions!

Observation, Professional Judgement, Recognition and Identification

THIS SECTION CONTAINS SELF-ASSESSMENT QUESTIONS AND TUTORIALS. The tutorials are designed to familiarize general principles and the self-assessment contains general questions similar to the questions likely to be on the exam, but are not intended to be identical to the exam questions. If you do not understand parts of the tutorial, or find the tutorial difficult, it is recommended that you seek out additional instruction.

The questions in the self-assessment are not the same as you will find on the exam - that would be too easy! And nobody knows what the questions will be and they change all the time. Mostly, the changes consist of substituting new questions for old, but the changes also can be new question formats or styles, changes to the number of questions in each section, changes to the time limits for each section, and combining sections. So the format and exact wording of the questions may differ slightly, and changes from year to year, if you can answer the questions below, you will have no problem with the questions on the RCMP Entrance Exam.

Observation Self-Assessment

Directions: You have five minutes to memorize the following information. Do not write anything down. Questions follow on page 56.

Name: Angela Jones
Description: 5 ft. 2 in. Black Canadian with long frizzy hair. No other identifying features.

Wanted For: Fraud

Name: Ryan McPherson
Description: 5 ft 8 in. Brown hair, clean-cut. Earring in right ear.

Wanted For: Bank Robbery

Make/Model: Unkown
Color: Red
License Plate: AJ1 26K British Columbia
Wanted in Connection with: Armed Robbery

Make/Model: Chevrolet Impala
Color: Yellow
License Plate: ARU-8364 Alberta
Wanted in Connection with: Assault

Observation Set II

Name: Mike Johnson
Description: 5 ft. 8 in Short hair and clean-cut. No other identifying features.

Wanted For: Trafficking

Name: Bryson Strong
Description: 5 ft. 5 in Short hair and clean cut. Scar on left fore-head.

Wanted For: Drunk and Disorderly

Make/Model: Mini Cooper
Color: 2-tone Turquoise and White
License Plate: AMCR-834 Ontario
Wanted in Connection with: Vehicular Homicide

Make/Model: Peugeot Coupe
Color: Green
License Plate: A52 BCP Quebec
Wanted in Connection with: Stolen Vehicle

Memorization and Memory Tricks

If you are going to master the art of studying, you are going to have to master one of life's basic skills: memorization. Do not panic! It is not as hard as you might think. Learning a few basic memorization techniques will give you the skills you need to make learning and retaining information a cinch.

Repeat, Repeat, Repeat. Repetition is a clever way of convincing your brain that the material you are studying is important. That is because, when an idea, a person, or an event is important to you, your mind will return to it again and again. By constantly and consistently reviewing new material, you will lock in the facts that you need to remember. Put simply, repetition saturates your brain with facts, words, and ideas to the point that you can't help but remember them later when you need them for a test.

Say It Out Loud. Verbalizing the information that you are studying is another way to imbed it into your mind. Speaking the words aloud is like a double repetition, because you are simultaneously speaking them and hearing them. This involves your brain in yet another way, increasing the likelihood that you will remember the facts when you need them. As well, saying the words aloud actually teaches your mouth to recognize them. When you are trying to recall the information and can remember a phrase, whispering it tonics yourself can bring the entire piece of information right back into your mind.

Make Connections. Humor is a useful tool to help you memorize a fact that just isn't sticking. Instead of looking at the information logically and intellectually, consider it in terms of associations or images. For example, let's say you are trying to learn the definition of 'scoliosis.' The word means curvature of the spine. You might notice that the letter's' occurs three times, and that this letter is a curvy one. It is also the first letter in the word 'spine.' When you see the word on a test, you will recognize the curving letters and remember the association with 'spine!'

When you create a strange association, your brain sees this

as something out of the ordinary. The brain has a sense of humor, and enjoys making puns, putting together unusual images and, otherwise having fun with language and ideas. It remembers things that are out of the ordinary more than it does the commonplace. So the more bizarre that you make this combination, the better your chance of recalling the information.

Keep in mind that using only one of these suggestions in and of itself is not the ultimate key to memorization. If a technique doesn't work for a particular bit of information, try another. You can even combine a couple of approaches. The more you use these strategies, the more likely your brain is to agree with you that the material you are studying is not only worth remembering, it is actually enjoyable.

Following are some additional strategies to help you memorize material. Try different ones and see what sticks the best for you.

Using Mnemonics

Mnemonics are tricks to help you remember information. Mnemonics come in several varieties, allowing you to choose what clicks for you. Some mnemonics enjoy widespread use because they are easy and effective, but you can always make up your own.

Visual Mnemonics– Visual mnemonics involve creating images that somehow suggest the information that is to be remembered. The image might be connected to the information in some logical way, or it can be completely unrelated. For example, if you are trying to remember that an event took place in Chillicothe, Ohio, you could visualize a cup of coffee sitting in a freezer (chilly coffee). Imaging a map of the state of Ohio on the coffee much will to help you in remembering that Chillicothe is in Ohio.

Visual mnemonics can be useful in learning another language as well. For example, rey is the Spanish word for king or monarch. Visualizing a crown with rays of light coming out from it reinforces the meaning with a mental image. The Spanish verb caminar means 'to walk,' so you could visualize an old El Camino model of car that is broken down, forcing you to walk.

Acronyms – Acronyms use the letters in a phrase or sentence to create an easy-to-remember word. A well-known example of this is ROY G. BIV. The letters stand for red, orange, yellow, green, blue, indigo and violet, which are the colors of the spectrum in order. This technique can be combined with a visual mnemonic to further lock it in. Imagining a cartoon character names Roy G. BIV, who wears a red hat, has orange hair, a yellow tie, a green shirt, a blue belt, indigo pants and a violet shirt makes the information you are trying to memorize impossible to forget!

A variation of the acronym mnemonic is to use the letters to create a simple sentence. With the spectrum colors, 'Richard of York Gave Battle in Vain' can serve as a memory device. Creating a simple song to go along with a sentence mnemonic makes remembering the words a tad easier.

Here is an example for anyone who is studying biology and needs to know taxonomy classifications. By looking at the first letters of each word in the acronym 'Kids Prefer Cheese Over Fried Green Spinach,' it is easy to remember Kingdom, Phylum, Class, Order, Family, Genus, Species, and these are the taxonomy classifications in order.

Acronyms can be used for any subject, including math. For example, at first glance pi seems like a hopelessly long string of numbers that is nearly impossible to memorize. However, the acronym 'How I wish I could calculate pi' is all you need to know. Here, the acronym isn't based on the first letter of each word, but on the number of letters in each word. The first word, 'how' has three letters. 'I' is a single letter, while 'wish' is a four-letter word. These are the first 3 numbers in pi—3.14. The number of letters in each word represents one digit of pi, giving you 3.141592. Memorizing a simple, fun phrase can save a lot of time and brain power.

Taking a Mnemonic Journey – Also known as the Method of Loci, journey mnemonics simply involve taking a mental journey with the information you are trying to integrate. As you study, imagine yourself walking through a familiar area. Picture words or images that represent the information superimposed on or featured in a particular location along the journey. For example, if you are studying art history, you might imagine yourself walking through your home, from the entrance to the bedroom. Throughout your walk, visualize famous paintings or sculptures along the walls, floor, or in the doorways. Take the mental walk a few times to really lock in the information. By mentally retracing those steps during the art history exam, the art work and artists will be easy to recall.

This method does not have to be used with paintings, sculptures or other obviously visual items. You can combine it with one or more other techniques and apply them to any subject. Picturing something in a specific location that you know well will help reinforce the connection. For example, the crown with rays of light coming out of it may be hanging on your bedpost, while the El Camino is parked outside your window.

Word Play – Rhymes and catchy phrases are an excellent mnemonic approach for adults as well as for children. They do not have to be complicated and can be used for any subject. Some rhymes have been so ingrained in us that decades after learning them, they come back to help us remember how to spell a word or recall a fact. Remembering the spelling mnemonic, 'I before E, except after C, or when sounded like A, as in neighbor and weigh,' has helped many a child—and adult--manage difficult spelling challenges. Remembering the meanings of the homonyms 'there,' 'their,' and 'they're' is made easier by recalling the catchy phrase, 'Here' is in 'there', 'heir' is in 'their', and they're just means they are. This one works because both 'here' and 'there' are locations, while 'their' refers to possession, and an 'heir' inherits possessions. You can create a little rhyme to explain all kinds of words you have trouble remembering how to spell. For example, 'There are three e's buried in the cemetery' helps unblock confusion about which vowel to use.

Associations – Another way to remember something is to associate the information with something easier to recall.

While associations can be loosely grouped with other types of mnemonics, they are actually a little different. For example, many people have difficulty remembering the difference between stalactites and stalagmites. Stalactites grow down from the cave's ceiling, and there is a 'c' in the middle of the word. Stalagmites, however, contains a 'g', and since they grow up from the ground, that 'g' can stand for 'ground.' Confusing dessert and desert is a very common mistake, but it is easy to create an association to help you remember the difference. For example, the Sahara is a famous desert, and both words contain a single 's.' Another word for dessert is sweets, and both of those words contain two letters 's.'

Associations do not have to be based on spelling. For a physical example on how associations can work, take a look at your hands. You are going to use the knuckles and the spaces between them as association points to the months in the year. Starting with your left pinky knuckle, name the months. The months that fall in the spaces between the knuckles have 30 days, except for February. Those that land on the knuckles are months can contain 31 days. For this trick to work, skip the valley between thumb and index fingers and jump to the right hand's index knuckle, since July and August have 31 days. Another physical mnemonic useful for teaching youngsters how to remember which is their right hand and which the left involves forming an 'L' with the thumb and index finger of the left hand. The 'L' is going in the correct direction, so that is the left hand.

Memory tricks can make studying a much easier process, regardless of your age. They do not have to be logical, sensible or even related to your subject, and your favorites may not work for other people. The trick is to make sure the mnemonics you use are ones that work for you.

Scenario 1

Dispatch reports a complaint of noisy and unruly teenagers hanging on the street. You proceed immediately to the area alone. You park the car nearby and observe 10 or 12 teens on the sidewalk. They do not appear to be taking drugs or drinking.

1. What should you do first?

a. Approach the group and arrest them right away.

b. Call for backup.

c. Return to the station as there are no crimes being committed.

d. Approach and question the group alone.

Scenario 2

2. Dispatch replies that back up is on its way. You wait in the car until 2 officers arrive. What is your next course of action.

a. Approach the group with the 2 backup officers and politely inform them there has been a noise complaint.

b. With the back up officers, arrest all the teens.

c. Approach the group alone with the two backup officers still in the car, and tell the group they will have to be more quiet.

d. Divide the group into three and have each officer question one group.

3. The teenagers are a little hostile but are not committing any crime. What should you do?

a. Arrest all of them.

b. Repeat that there has been a noise complaint, and ask them to please be more quiet.

c. Search the group for drugs.

d. Leave the scene.

Scenario 3

You are called to a street lamp that has fallen across the street, partly blocking traffic. You are the first to arrive.

4. What is the first action that you should take?

a. Report the fallen lamp to dispatch.

b. Check the street lamp for exposed or loose wires that may be carrying current.

c. Secure the area around the fallen street lamp with pylons to direct traffic around the lamp and give dispatch an update on the situation.

d. Evacuate the neighborhood.

Scenario 4

5. You recognize a stolen car and confirm with dispatch you are following the car alone. The stolen car has 4 people in it and you are alone. What should you do?

a. Pull the car over immediately

b. Call for backup, giving your position and situation, and keep following the car

c. Report the position and direction and stop following the car.

d. Call for backup and keep following the car.

Scenario 5

6. You are called to a robbery and see two cars leaving the scene at high speed. You give chase, however, the cars are driving at very high speed and driving very dangerously.

What should you do?

a. Call dispatch with as much information as possible

b. Follow the cars and match their speed.

c. Follow the cars at a high but safe speed, even if you fall behind

c. Follow the cars but do not exceed the speed limit.

Answer Key

1. B
The safest course of action is to call for backup.

2. A
A low key and polite approach is best.

3. B
No crime is being committed, so there is no reason to arrest, and searching may antagonize them and the situation could deteriorate quickly if handled aggressively.

4. C
The first priority is to ensure safety and secure the area, then give dispatch an updated report. Inspecting the street light, beyond a quick inspection, is beyond your expertise and not your job. Better to wait for qualified people to arrive.

5. B
With four people in the car, pulling them over alone is not advised. The priority is to give dispatch the most information you can and keep following the car.

6. C
One of your responsibilities is the safety, which includes yourself. In addition, a high speed chase could endanger innocent people. The best action is to follow the cars at a high but safe speed and update dispatch with a description of the cars and any other information you have.

How to Answer this type of Question

Answering professional judgement questions involves common sense and following a set of basic criteria.

1. Safety - Assisting victims of crime, and injured persons.

This is first and foremost the most important duty. Assisting injured persons, includes other officers.

2. Following Instructions

In an emergency, others, who may see a larger picture that you cannot, are counting on you to follow their orders without question.

3. Protect Property - calming disorder

Protecting private and public property and calming disorder and one for key duties of a police officer.

4. Perform duties - Keep the Peace, enforce the law, maintain order.

Keeping the peace and enforcing the law are the primary duties of a police officer.

Observation Answer Key (From Page 40 - 43)

1. What is the name of the African Canadian wanted for fraud?

a. Ryan McPherson
b. Angela Jones
c. Bryson Strong
d. Mike Johnson

2. What Province is the car wanted in connection with armed robbery from?

a. Alberta
b. Quebec
c. British Columbia
d. Ontario

3. What model is the Chevrolet from Alberta?

a. Impala
b. Malibu
c. Caprice
d. Lumina

4. Who is wanted for trafficking?

a. Bryson Strong
b. Mike Johnson
c. Angela Jones
d. Ryan McPherson

5. What is the Mini Cooper wanted for?

a. Stolen vehicle
b. Vehicular homicide
c. Armed Robbery
d. Assault

6. What Province is the Peugeot Coupe from?

a. Alberta
b. Quebec
c. British Columbia
d. Ontario

Answer Key

1. B

Angela Jones is the Black Canadian.

2. C

The red car, unknown model and make wanted for armed robbery is from British Columbia.

3. A

The Chevrolet model is an Impala.

4. B

Mike Johnson is wanted for trafficking.

5. B

The Mini Cooper is wanted in connection with a vehicular homicide.

6. B

The Peugeot Coupe is from Quebec.

Recognition and Identification

THIS SECTION CONTAINS A SELF-ASSESSMENT AND A SHORT RECOGNITION AND IDENTIFICATION TUTORIAL. The tutorials are designed to familiarize general principles and the self-assessment contains general questions similar to the questions likely to be on the RCMP, but are not intended to be identical to the exam questions.

The questions below are not the same as you will find on the RCMP - that would be too easy! And nobody knows what the questions will be and they change all the time. Mostly the changes consist of substituting new questions for old, but the changes can be new question formats or styles, changes to the number of questions in each section, changes to the time limits for each section and combining sections. Below are general quantitative skills questions that cover the same areas as the RCMP. So the format and exact wording of the questions may differ slightly, and change from year to year, if you can answer the questions below, you will have no problem with this section of the RCMP entrance test.

1. Choose the person that matches the suspect below.

2. Choose the person that matches the suspect below.

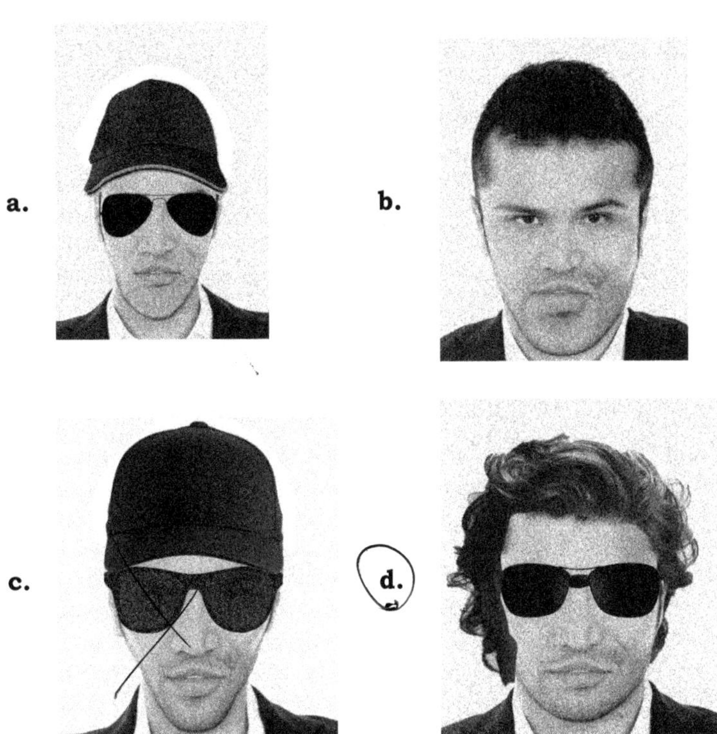

a.

b.

c.

d.

Answer Key

1. A

Choice A is the same person. Choice B looks like a good choice as they are both wearing hoodies - notice though, the cheek bones are much narrower. Choices C and D are different people - the shape of their heads is quite different.

2. D

Choice D is the same person with different hair and sunglasses. Choices A and C have narrower facial structure. Choice B has a wider facial structure.

How to answer this type of question.

Like most (all) types of questions on the RCMP exam, practice practice practice! In recognizing and identifying a suspect, focus on what can't be changed - eye color, cheek bones, facial structure, identifying marks such as birthmarks. Tattoos and piercings are also a clue, though they leave a mark and can be covered up.

Here is an example:

Choose the person that matches the suspect below.

Facial Structure is noticeably thinner so it can't be the same person.

Facial structure is much wider so it can't be the same person.

Facial Structure is the same - clearly the same person wearing sunglasses.

Composition

THIS SECTION CONTAINS A COMPOSITION SELF-ASSESSMENT. The tutorials are designed to familiarize general principles and the self-assessment contains general questions similar to the composition questions likely to be on the exam, but are not intended to be identical to the exam questions. The tutorials are not designed to be a complete course, and it is assumed that students have some familiarity with English grammar and usage. If you do not understand parts of the tutorial, or find the tutorial difficult, it is recommended that you seek out additional instruction.

Tour of the Composition Content

Below is a detailed list of the topics likely to appear on the exam.

- Spelling
- Vocabulary
- English usage
- English grammar

The questions in the self-assessment are not the same as you will find on the exam - that would be too easy! And nobody knows what the questions will be and they change all the time. Mostly, the changes consist of substituting new questions for old, but the changes also can be new question formats or styles, changes to the number of questions in each section, changes to the time limits for each section, and combining sections. So the format and exact wording of the questions may differ slightly, and changes from year to year, if you can answer the questions below, you will have

Fill in the Blanks

1. Our ______ to America by sea was not very comfortable.

a. journey
b. voyage
c. travel
d. none of the above

2. I do not want to ______ a friend like you.

a. lose
b. loose
c. lost
d. none of the above

3. This pain killer will ______ your pain.

a. lesson
b. lessen
c. lesen
d. leson

4. Collecting stamps, ____________________ and listening to shortwave radio were Rick's main hobbies.

a. building models
b. to build models
c. having built models
d. build models

Directions: Choose the correct version of the underlined word or phrase in the given sentence.

5. She is the <u>most cleverest</u> girl in the class.

a. She is the most clever girl in the class.
b. She is the cleverest girl in the class.
c. She is the most cleverer girl in the class.
d. None of the above.

6. He <u>lived</u> in California since 1995.

a. He had lived in California since 1995.
b. He has been living in California since 1995.
c. He has living in California since 1995.
d. None of the above.

7. Politics <u>are</u> his chief interest.

a. Politics is his chief interest.
b. Politics are his chief interests.
c. Politics is his chief interests.
d. The sentence is correct.

8. He is a <u>cowered</u> person.

a. He is a cowardest person.
b. He is a cowardly person.
c. He is a coward person.
d. The sentence is correct.

9. Choose the sentence with the correct grammar.

a. The man was asked to come with his daughter and her test results.

b. The man was asked to come with her daughter and her test results.

c. The man was asked to come with her daughter and our test results.

d. None of the above.

10. Choose the sentence with the correct grammar.

a. Neither of them came with their bicycle.

b. Neither of them came with his bicycle.

c. Neither of them came with our bicycle.

d. None of the above.

11. Choose the correct spelling.

a. Weather

b. Weathur

c. Wether

d. None of the above

12. Choose the correct spelling.

a. Withdrawl

b. Withdrawal

c. Withdrawel

d. Witdrawal

13. Choose the correct spelling.

a. Yatch

b. Yache

c. Yaute

d. Yacht

14. Choose the correct spelling.

a. Yeild
b. Yielde
c. Yield
d. Yeelde

15. Choose the correct spelling.

a. Warrant
b. Warrent
c. Warent
d. Warant

16. Choose the correct spelling.

a. Thorou
b. Thurough
c. Thorough
d. Thorogh

17. Choose the correct spelling.

a. Tomorow
b. Tomorrow
c. Tommorow
d. Tommorrow

18. Choose the correct spelling.

a. Unicke
b. Uniqe
c. Unique
d. None of the Above

19. Choose the correct spelling.

a. Unice
b. Usable
c. Ussable
d. Usabble

20. Choose the correct spelling.

a. Usually
b. Usualy
c. Ususally
d. Ussually

Fill in the Blank.

21. When Joe broke his ______ in a skiing accident, his entire leg was in a cast.

a. Ankle
b. Humerus
c. Wrist
d. Femur

22. Alan had to learn the _____ system of numbering when his family moved to Great Britain.

a. American
b. Decimal
c. Metric
d. Fingers and toes

23. After Lisa's aunt had her tenth child, Lisa found that she had more than twenty _______.

a. Uncles
b. Friends
c. Stepsisters
d. Cousins

24. She was a rabid Red Sox fan, attending every game, and demonstrating her _________ by cheering more loudly than anyone else.

a. Knowledge
b. Boredom
c. Commitment
d. Enthusiasm

25. When Craig's dog was struck by a car, he rushed his pet to the ___________.

a. Emergency room
b. Doctor
c. Veterinarian
d. Podiatrist

26. Gasoline is very ________.

a. Volatile
b. Flammable
c. Inert
d. None of the above

27. The tree has ________ over millions of years.

a. Scared
b. Petrified
c. Rotted
d. None of the above

28. They always get along and never ________.

a. Bicker
b. Socialize
c. Debate
d. None of the above

29. Her reputation as a ________ often gets her into trouble.

a. Maverick
b. Conformist
c. Insider
d. None of the above

30. Don't worry it will ______ in a few minutes.

a. Degenerate
b. Dissipate
c. Scatter
d. None of the above

Answer Key

1. B
"Travel" is a verb meaning to go from one place to another. A "journey" is a noun that refers to the travel event. A "voyage" is a journey by sea.

2. A
"Lose" is a verb meaning to misplace something or to fail at a competition. "Loose" is an adjective meaning untied or able to move freely.

3. B
"Lessen" means to reduce in size or intensity. "Lesson" refers to a formal time period in which particular information is taught or learned.

4. A
Present progressive "building models" is correct in this sentence.

5. B
Cleverest is the proper form to express 'most clever.'

6. B
Past perfect continuous, has been living, is proper because the time element, since 1995, and he is still living there now.

7. A
In spite of the 's' ending, "politics" is a singular noun.

8. B
"Cowardly" is an adjective used to modify a person.

9. A
A Pronoun should conform to its antecedent in gender, number and person.

10. B
Words such as neither, each, many, either, every, everyone, everybody and any should take a singular pronoun. Here we are assuming that the subject is male, and so use "his."

The subject could be female, in which case we would use "her," however that is not one of the choices here.

11. A
Weather is the correct spelling.

12. B
Withdrawal is the correct spelling.

13. D
Yacht is the correct spelling.

14. C
Yield is the correct spelling.

15. A
Warrant is the correct spelling.

16. C
Thorough is the correct spelling.

17. B
Tomorrow is the correct spelling.

18. C
Unique is the correct spelling.

19. B
Usable is the correct spelling.

20. A
Usually is the correct spelling.

21. D
Femur NOUN the bone of the thigh or upper hind limb, articulating at the hip and the knee.

22. C
Metric System NOUN the decimal measuring system based on the meter, liter, and gram as units of length, capacity, and weight or mass.

23. D
Cousin NOUN a child of one's uncle or aunt.

24. D
Enthusiasm NOUN intense and eager enjoyment, interest, or approval.

25. C
Veterinarian NOUN a person quali ied to treat diseased or injured animals.

26. A
Volatile liable to change rapidly and unpredictably, especially for the worse.

27. B
Petrified ADJECTIVE changed to stone

28. A
Bicker VERB to quarrel in a tiresome, insulting manner.

29. A
Maverick NOUN showing independence in thoughts or actions.

30. B
Dissipate VERB to disperse or scatter.

English Grammar and Punctuation Tutorials

Capitalization

Although many of the rules for capitalization are pretty straight forward, there are several tricky points that are important to review.

Starting a Sentence

Everyone knows that you need to capitalize the first letter of the first word in a sentence, but is it really all that easy to figure out where one sentence starts and another stops? Take these three examples:

That was the moment it really sunk in: There would be no hockey this year.

It was April and that could mean only one thing: baseball.

We played for hours before heading home; everyone felt tired and happy.

In thc first example the first letter after the colon is capitalized while in the second example it is not. That is because everything after the first example's colon is a complete sentence, while after example two's colon there is only one word. In example three you have what could be a complete sentence ("everyone felt tired and happy"), but which is not because it follows a semicolon, making it just another clause instead.

Essentially, within a sentence you can have an additional complete sentence if the sentence follows a colon. However, if what could be a complete sentence follows a semicolon, it is a clause and does not get capitalized.

Remember that the same rules apply for quotation marks

that apply for colons: A complete sentence inside quotation marks is capitalized, but a single word or phrase is not.

Proper Nouns

The first letter of all proper nouns needs to be capitalized. There are many categories of proper noun. The most common proper nouns are the specific names of people (such as Bill), places (such as Germany) or things (such as Honda Civic). However, there are several less obvious categories of words that should be capitalized as proper nouns.

Historical events such as World War II or the California Gold Rush need to be capitalized.

The names of celestial bodies such as Orion's Belt need to be capitalized.

The names of ethnicities such as African-American or Hispanic need to be capitalized.

Relationship words that replace a person's name such as Mom, Doctor and Mister need to be capitalized. However, this only happens when you use the word to replace the person's name. In the sentence, "My mom went to the store," you do not capitalize it, while in the sentence, "Hey Mom, did you get toothpaste at the store?" you do capitalize it.

Geographical locations are capitalized. This can get a little tricky because capitalized geographical locations and non-capitalized directions are easy to confuse. Saying, "We drove south for hours," is a direction, so the word "south" should not be capitalized. But when saying, "While in the United States, we drove to the South to look at Civil War battle fields," you do capitalize the word "South." The difference is that in the first sentence "south" is just the direction you drove. In the second sentence "the South" is a specific region of the United States that formed itself into the Confederacy during the US Civil War.

Proper Adjectives

Proper adjectives are the adjective forms of proper nouns. People from Germany are German; people from Canada are Canadian. German and Canadian are proper adjectives because they are forms of proper nouns that are used to describe other nouns.

Titles of Works

Titles of works are generally capitalized following a specific pattern. Capitalize all of the important words in a sentence. Do not capitalize unimportant words such as prepositions and articles.

For example: Alien Spaceship Spotted over Many of the World's Capitals

Notice that the prepositions "over" and "of," and the article "the" are the only non-capitalized words in the sentence.

Colons and Semicolons

Within a sentence there are several different types of punctuation marks that can denote a pause. Each of these punctuation marks has different rules when it comes to its structure and usage, so we will look at each one in turn.

Colons

The colon is used primarily to introduce information. It can start lists such as in the sentence, "There were several things Susan had to get at the store: bread, cereal, lettuce and tomatoes." Or a colon can be used to point out specific information, such as in the sentence, "It was only then that the group fully realized what had happened: The Martian invasion had begun."

Note that if the information after the colon is a complete sentence, you capitalize and punctuate it exactly like you would a sentence. If, however, it does not constitute a complete sentence, you don't have to capitalize anything. ("Peering out the window Meredith saw them: zombies.")

Semicolons

Semicolons can be thought of as super commas. They denote a stronger stop than a comma does, but they are still weaker than a period, not quite capable of ending a sentence. Semicolons are primarily used to separate independent clauses that are not being separated by a coordinating conjunction. ("Chris went to the store; he bought chips and salsa.") Semicolons can only do this, however, when the ideas in each clause are related. For instance, the sentence, "It's raining outside; my sister went to the movies," is not a proper usage of the semicolon since those clauses have nothing to do with each other.

Semicolons can also be used in lists provided that one or more element in the list is itself made up of a smaller list. If you want to write a list of things you plan to bring to a picnic, and those things only include a Frisbee, a chair and some pasta salad, you would not need to use a semicolon. But if you also wanted to bring plastic knives, forks and spoons, you would need to write your sentence like this: "For our picnic I am bringing a Frisbee; a chair; plastic knives, forks and spoons; and some pasta salad."

Using semicolons like this preserves the smaller list that you have in your larger list.

Commas

Commas are probably the most commonly used punctuation mark in English. Commas can break the flow of writing to give it a more natural sounding style, and they are the main punctuation mark used to separate ideas. Commas also separate lists, introductory adverbs, introductory prepositional phrases, dates and addresses.

The most rigid way that commas are used is when separating clauses. There are two primary types of clauses in a sentence, independent and subordinate (sometimes called dependent). Independent clauses are clauses that express a complete thought, such as, "Tim went to the store." Subordinate clauses, on the other hand, only express partial thoughts that expand on an independent clause such as, "after the game ended," which you can see is clearly not a complete sentence. (You will learn more about clauses in different lessons.)

The rule for commas with clauses is that a comma must separate the clauses when a subordinate clause comes first in a sentence: "After the game ended, Tim went to the store." But there should not be a comma when a subordinate clause follows an independent clause: "Tim went to the store after the game ended." If you leave the comma out of the first example, you have a run-on sentence. If you add one into the second example, you have a comma-splice error. Also, when you have two independent clauses joined with a coordinating conjunction, you need to separate them with a comma. "Tim went to the store, and Beth went home."

There are some artistic exceptions to these rules, such as adding a pause for literary effect, but for the most part, they are set in stone.

Commas are also used to separate items in a list. This area of English is unfortunately less clear than it should be, with two separate rules depending on what standard you are following. To understand the two different rules, let's pretend you are having a party at your house, and you are making a list of refreshments your friends will want. You may decide to serve three things: 1) pizza 2) chips 3) drinks. There are two different rules governing how you should punctuate this. According to many grammar books, you would write this as, "At the store I will buy pizza, chips, and drinks."

This variation puts a comma after each item in the list. It is the version that the style books used in most college English and history courses will prefer, so it is probably the one you should follow. However, the Associated Press style guide, which is used in college journalism classes and at newspapers and magazines, says the sentence should be written like this: "At the store I will buy pizza, chips and drinks." Here you only use a comma between the first two words, letting the word "and" act as the separator between the last two.

Another important place to use commas is when you have a modifier that describes an element of a sentence, but that does not directly follow the thing it describes. Look at the sentence: "Tim went over to visit Beth, watching the full moon along the way." In this sentence there is no confusion about who is "watching the full moon"; it is Tim, probably as he walks to Beth's house. If you remove the comma, however, you get this: "Tim went over to visit Beth watching the full moon along the way." Now it sounds as though Beth is watching the full moon, and we are forced to wonder what "way" the moon is traveling along.

Commas are also used when adding introductory prepositional phrases and introductory adverbs to sentences. A comma is always needed following an introductory adverb. ("Quickly, Jody ran to the car.") Commas are even necessary when you have an adverb introducing a clause within a sentence, even if the clause not the first clause of the sentence. ("Amanda wanted to go to the movie; however, she knew her homework was more important.")

With introductory prepositional phrases you only add a comma if the phrase (or if a group of introductory phrases) is five or more words long. Thus, the sentence you just read did not have a comma following its introductory prepositional phrase ("With introductory prepositional phrases") because it was only four words. Compare that to this sentence with a five word introductory phrase: "After the ridiculously long class, the friends needed to relax."

The last way commas are used in sentences is to separate information that does not need to be there. For instance, "My cousin Hector, who wore a blue hat at the party, thought you were funny." The fact that Hector wore a blue hat is interesting, but it is not vital to the sentence; it could be removed and not changed the sentence's meaning. Therefore, it gets commas around it. Along these lines you should remember that any clause introduced by the word that is considered to provide essential information to the sentence and should not get commas around it. Conversely, any clause starting with the word which is considered nonessential and should not get commas around it.

Quotation Marks

Quotation marks are used in English in a variety of different ways. The most common use of quotation marks is to show quotations either, as dialogue or, when directly quoting a source in an essay or news article. Fortunately, both of these uses follow the same basic rules.

When you have a quote written as the second part of a sentence, you need to put a comma before the quotation marks and a period inside the quotation marks at the end. (Franklin said, “Let’s go to the store.”) Conversely, when you have quote as the first part of the sentence with information describing it second, a comma replaces the period at the end of the sentence inside the quotes. (“Let’s go to the store,” Franklin said.)

If the information in a quote is not a complete sentence you do not need to capitalize it or put commas around it, if it is not dialogue. (No one thought the idea of “going to the store” sounded very fun.)

Note that when the last word in a sentence has both a quotation mark and a period attached to it, the period is always inside the quotes. This is the case when you have a complete sentence inside a quote (“Let’s go to the store.”), and when the last word in a sentence just happens to have quote marks around it (Kerri said I was “mean.”) You also need to do the same thing with commas. (Kerri said I was “mean,” and it made me feel bad.) However, other punctuation marks such as colons, semicolons and dashes do not follow this rule and should come outside the quotes. (Kerri said I was “mean”; it made me feel bad.)

When you want to use a quote inside a quote, you use the

standard double-quotation marks for the outer quote and single-quotation marks for the inner quote. ("The sign on the door said 'no soliciting,' so we went to the next house.")

Quotation marks are also used around certain types of titles. To figure out which ones, it helps to look at which titles are not put in quotes as well.

Titles are generally broken down into two categories: large works and small works. Large works are things such as newspapers, magazines, CDs, books and television shows. The defining characteristic of a large work is that it is able to hold small works in it. Small works are the articles inside newspapers and magazines, the songs on a CD, the chapters in a book and the episodes of a television show. It is small works that get quotation marks around them. (Large works, meanwhile, are either underlined or italicized.)

Using quotation marks correctly in a title looks something like this: The two-page article entitled "San Francisco Giants Win World Series" appeared in yesterday's New York Times. The article title is in quotes, and the newspaper title is in italics.

Common English Usage Mistakes - A Quick Review

Like some parts of English grammar, usage is definitely going to be on the exam and there isn't any tricky strategies or shortcuts to help you get through this section.

Here is a quick review of common usage mistakes.

1. May and Might

'May' can act as a principal verb, which can express permission or possibility.

Examples:

Lets wait, the meeting may have started.
May I begin now?

'May' can act as an auxiliary verb, which an expresses a purpose or wish

Examples:

May you find favour in the sight of your employer.
May your wishes come true.
People go to school so that they may be educated.

The past tense of may is might.

Examples:

I asked if I might begin

'Might' can be used to signify a weak or slim possibility or polite suggestion.

Examples:

You might find him in his office, but I doubt it.
You might offer to help if you want to.

2. Lie and Lay

The verb lay should always take an object. The three forms of the verb lay are: laid, lay and laid.

The verb lie (recline) should not take any object. The three forms of the verb lie are: lay, lie and lain.

Examples:

Lay on the bed.

The tables were laid by the students.
Let the little kid lie.
The patient lay on the table.

The dog has lain there for 30 minutes.

Note: The verb lie can also mean "to tell a falsehood." This verb can appear in three forms: lied, lie, and lied. This is different from the verb lie (recline) mentioned above.

Examples:

The accused is fond of telling lies.
Did she lie?

3. Would and should

The past tense of shall is 'should', and so "should" generally follows the same principles as "shall."

The past tense of will is "would," and so "would" generally follows the same principles as "will."

The two verbs 'would and should' can be correctly used interchangeably to signify obligation. The two verbs also have some unique uses too. Should is used in three persons to signify obligation.

Examples:

I should go after work.
People should do exercises everyday.
You should be generous.

"Would" is specially used in any of the three persons, to signify willingness, determination and habitual action.

Examples:

They would go for a test run every Saturday.
They would not ignore their duties.
She would try to be punctual.

4. Principle and Auxiliary Verbs

Two principal verbs can be used along with one auxiliary verb as long as the auxiliary verb form suits the two principal verbs.

Examples:

A number of people have been employed and some promoted.

A new tree has been planted and the old has been cut down.

Again note the difference in the verb form.

5. Can and Could

A. Can is used to express capacity or ability.

Examples:

I can complete the assignment today
He can meet up with his target.

B. Can is also used to express permission.

Examples:

Yes, you can begin

In the sentence below, "can" was used to mean the same thing as "may." However, the difference is that the word "can" is used for negative or interrogative sentences, while "may" is used in affirmative sentences to express possibility.

Examples:

They may be correct. Positive sentence - use may.
Can this statement be correct? A question using "can."
It cannot be correct. Negative sentence using "can."

The past tense of can is could. It can serve as a principal verb when it is used to express its own meaning.

Examples:

In spite of the difficulty of the test, he could still perform well.
"Could" here is used to express ability.

6. Ought

The verb ought should normally be followed by the word to.

Examples:

I *ought to* close shop now.

The verb 'ought' can be used to express:

A. Desirability

You ought to wash your hands before eating. It is desirable to wash your hands.

B. Probability

She ought to be on her way back by now. She is probably on her way.

C. Moral obligation or duty

The government ought to protect the oppressed. It is the government's duty to protect the oppressed.

7. Raise and Rise

Rise

The verb rise means to go up, or to ascend.
The verb rise can appear in three forms, rose, rise, and risen. The verb should not take an object.

Examples:

The bird rose very slowly.
The trees rise above the house.
My aunt has risen in her career.

Raise

The verb raise means to increase, to lift up.
The verb raise can appear in three forms, raised, raise and raised.

Examples:

He raised his hand.
The workers requested a raise.
Do not raise that subject.

8. Past Tense and Past Participle

Pay attention to the proper use these verbs: sing, show, ring, awake, fly, flow, begin, hang and sink.
Mistakes usually occur when using the past participle and past tense of these verbs as they are often mixed up.

Each of these verbs can appear in three forms:

Sing, Sang, Sung.
Show, Showed, Showed/Shown.
Ring, Rang, Rung.
Awake, awoke, awaken
Fly, Flew, Flown.
Flow, Flowed, Flowed.
Begin, Began, Begun.
Hang, Hanged, Hanged (a criminal)
Hang, Hung, Hung (a picture)
Sink, Sank, Sunk.

Examples:

The stranger rang the door bell. (simple past tense)
I have rung the door bell already. (past participle - an action completed in the past)

The stone sank in the river. (simple past tense)
The stone had already sunk. (past participle - an action completed in the past)

The meeting began at 4:00.

The meeting has begun.

9. Shall and Will

When speaking informally, the two can be used interchangeably. In formal writing, they must be used correctly.

"Will" is used in the second or third person, while "shall" is used in the first person. Both verbs are used to express a time or even in the future.

Examples:

I shall, We shall (First Person)

You will (Second Person)
They will (Third Person)

This principle however reverses when the verbs are to be used to express threats, determination, command, willingness, promise or compulsion. In these instances, will is now used in first person and shall in the second and third person.

Examples:

I will be there next week, no matter what.
This is a promise, so the first person "I" takes "will."

You shall ensure that the work is completed.
This is a command, so the second person "you" takes "shall."

I will try to make payments as promised.
This is a promise, so the first person "I" takes "will."

They shall have arrived by the end of the day.
This is a determination, so the third person "they" takes shall.

Note

A. The two verbs, shall and will, should not occur twice in the same sentence when the same future is being referred to

Example:

I shall arrive early if my driver is here on time.

B. Will should not be used in the first person when questions are being asked

Examples:

Shall I go?
Shall we go?

Subject Verb Agreement

Verbs in any sentence must agree with the subject of the sentence both in person and number. Problems usually occur when the verb doesn't correspond with the right subject or the verb fails to match the noun close to it.

Unfortunately, there is no easy way around these principals - no tricky strategy or easy rule. You just have to memorize them.

Here is a quick review:

The verb to be, present (past)

Person	Singular	Plural
First	I am (was)	we are (were)
Second	you are (were)	you are (were)
Third	he, she, it is (was)	they are (were)

The verb to have, present (past)

Person	Singular	Plural
First	I have (had)	we have (had)
Second	you have (had)	you have (had)
Third	he, she, it has (had)	they have (had)

Regular verbs, e.g. to walk, present (past)

Person	Singular	Plural
First	I walk (walked)	we walk (walked)
Second	you walk (walked)	you walk (walked)
Third	he, she, it walks (walked)	they work (walked)

1. Every and Each

When nouns are qualified by "every" or "each," they take a singular verb even if they are joined by 'and'

Examples:

Each mother and daughter was a given separate test.
Every teacher and student was properly welcomed.

2. Plural Nouns

Nouns like measles, tongs, trousers, riches, scissors etc. are all plural.

Examples:

The trousers are dirty.
My scissors have gone missing.
The tongs are on the table.

3. With and As Well

Two subjects linked by "with" or "as well" should have a verb that matches the first subject.

Examples:

The pencil, with the papers and equipment, is on the desk.
David as well as Louis is coming.

4. Plural Nouns

The following nouns take a singular verb:

> politics, mathematics, innings, news, advice, summons, furniture, information, poetry, machinery, vacation, scenery

Examples:

The machinery is difficult to assemble
The furniture has been delivered
The scenery was beautiful

5. Single Entities

A proper noun in plural form that refers to a single entity requires a singular verb. This is a complicated way of saying; some things appear to be plural, but are really singular, or some nouns refer to a collection of things but the collection is really singular.

Examples:

The United Nations Organization is the decision maker in the matter.

Here the "United Nations Organization" is really only one "thing" or noun, but is made up of many "nations."

The book, "The Seven Virgins" was not available in the library.
Here there is only one book, although the title of the book is plural.

6. Specific Amounts are always singular

A plural noun that refers to a specific amount or quantity that is considered as a whole (dozen, hundred, score etc) requires a singular verb.

Examples:

60 minutes is quite a long time.
Here "60 minutes" is considered a whole, and therefore one item (singular noun).

The first million is the most difficult.

7. Either, Neither and Each are always singular

The verb is always singular when used with: either, each, neither, everyone and many.

Examples:

Either of the boys is lying.
Each of the employees has been well compensated
Many a police officer has been found to be courageous
Every one of the teachers is responsible

8. Linking with Either, Or, and Neither match the second subject

Two subjects linked by "either," "or,""nor" or "neither" should have a verb that matches the second subject.

Examples:

Neither David nor Paul will be coming.
Either Mary or Tina is paying.

Note
If one subject linked by "either," "or,""nor" or "neither" is in plural form, then the verb should also be in plural, and the verb should be close to the plural subject.

Examples:
Neither the mother nor her kids have eaten.
Either Mary or her friends are paying.

9. Collective Nouns are Plural

Some collective nouns such as poultry, gentry, cattle, vermin etc. are considered plural and require a plural verb.

Examples:

The poultry are sick.
The cattle are well fed.

Note
Collective nouns involving people can work with both plural and singular verbs.
Examples:

Nigerians are known to be hard working
Europeans live in Africa

10. Nouns that are Singular and Plural

Nouns like deer, sheep, swine, salmon etc. can be singular or plural and require the same verb form.

Examples:

The swine is feeding. (singular)
The swine are feeding. (plural)

The salmon is on the table. (singular)
The salmon are running upstream. (plural)

11. Collective Nouns are Singular

Collective nouns such as Army, Jury, Assembly, Committee, Team etc should carry a singular verb when they subscribe to one idea. If the ideas or views are more than one, then the verb should be plural.

Examples:

The committee is in agreement in their decision.

The committee were in disagreement in their decision.
The jury has agreed on a verdict.
The jury were unable to agree on a verdict.

12. Subjects links by “and” are plural.

Two subjects linked by “and” always require a plural verb

Examples:

David and John are students.

Note
If the subjects linked by “and” are used as one phrase, or constitute one idea, then the verb must be singular

The color of his socks and shoe is black.
Here “socks and shoe” are two nouns, however the subject is “color” which is singular.

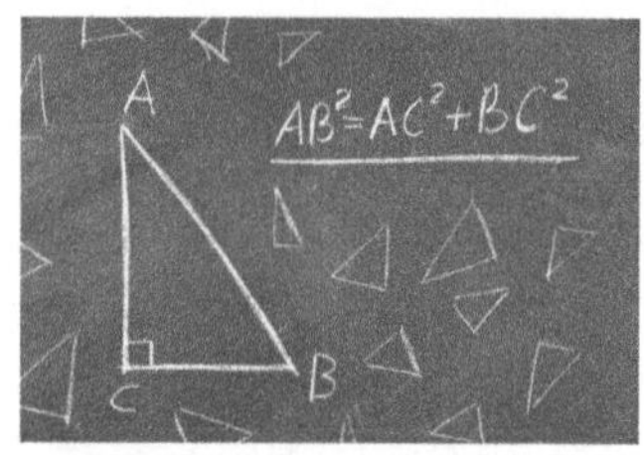

Mathematics

THIS SECTION CONTAINS A SELF-ASSESSMENT AND MATH TUTORIALS. The tutorials are designed to familiarize general principles and the self-assessment contains general questions similar to the math questions likely to be on the exam, but are not intended to be identical to the exam questions. The tutorials are not designed to be a complete math course, and it is assumed that students have some familiarity with math. If you do not understand parts of the tutorial, or find the tutorial difficult, it is recommended that you seek out additional instruction.

Tour of the RCMP Mathematics Content

Below is a detailed list of the mathematics topics likely to appear on the exam. Make sure that you understand these topics at the very minimum.

- Convert decimals, percent, roman numerals and fractions
- Solve word problems
- Calculate percent and ratio
- Operations using fractions, percent and fractions

- Analyze and interpret tables, graphs and charts
- Understand and solve simple algebra problems
- Simple Geometry

The questions in the self-assessment are not the same as you will find on the exam - that would be too easy! And nobody knows what the questions will be and they change all the time. Mostly, the changes consist of substituting new questions for old, but the changes also can be new question formats or styles, changes to the number of questions in each section, changes to the time limits for each section, and combining sections. So, while the format and exact wording of the questions may differ slightly, and changes from year to year, if you can answer the questions below, you will have no problem with the mathematics section .

Mathematics Self-Assessment

The purpose of the self-assessment is:

- Identify your strengths and weaknesses.
- Develop your personalized study plan (above)
- Get accustomed to the format
- Extra practice – the self-assessments are almost a full 3rd practice test!
- Provide a baseline score for preparing your study schedule.

Since this is a Self-assessment, and depending on how confident you are with Math, timing yourself is optional. This self-assessment has 15 questions, so allow about 15 minutes to complete.

Once complete, use the table below to assess your understanding of the content, and prepare your study schedule described in chapter 1.

80% - 100%	Excellent – you have mastered the content
60 – 79%	Good. You have a working knowledge. Even though you can just pass this section, you may want to review the tutorials and do some extra practice to see if you can improve your mark.
40% - 59%	Below Average. You do not understand the content. Review the tutorials , and retake this quiz again in a few days, before proceeding to the Practice Test Questions.
Less than 40%	Poor. You have a very limited understanding. Please review the tutorials , and retake this quiz again in a few days, before proceeding to the Practice Test Questions.

5. A boy has 5 red balls, 3 white balls and 2 yellow balls. What percent of the balls are yellow?

a. 2%
b. 8%
c. 20%
d. 12%

6. Add 10% of 300 to 50% of 20

a. 50%
b. 40%
c. 60%
d. 45%

7. Convert 75% to a fraction.

a. 2/100
b. 75/100
c. 3/4
d. 4/7

8. Convert 90% to a fraction

a. 1/10
b. 9/9
c. 10/100
d. 9/10

9. A man buys an item for $420 and has a balance of $3000.00. How much did he have before?

a. $2,580
b. $3,420
c. $2,420
d. $342

10. Divide 9.60 by 3.2

a. 2.50
b. 3
c. 2.3
d. 6.4

11. If X = 7 solve 3x + 5 – 2x

a. x = 6
b. x = 12
c. x = 1
d. x = 0

12. Solve √121

a. 11
b. 23
c. 12
d. 9

13. Solve 3x – 27 = 0

a. x = 24
b. x = 30
c. x = 9
d. x = 21

14. Solve the following equation 4(y + 6) = 3y + 30

a. y = 6
b. y = 20
c. y = 30/7
d. y = 30

15. Solve √144

a. 14
b. 72
c. 24
d. 12

Answer Key

1. B
First calculate the distance travelled in 1 minute.
100 km/hr. = 100/60 = 1.666 km/minute.
So, in 2 minutes the motorcycle will travel 3.33 ki eters.

2. B
For the first year, $4,000 invested at 8% will be 40 .08 = 320. The interest is compounded yearly, so to calc the second years interest, 4320 X .08 = 345.60.
The total will then be 4320 + 345.60 = $4665.60

3. C
First calculate her hourly wage. 6 hours X 10.50/ho $63. Next calculate tips. $240.60 X .12 = $28.87. S r total earnings will be 63 + 28.87 = 91.87

4. A
15% = 15/100 X 200 = 7.5%

5. C
Total no. of balls = 10, no. of yellow balls = 2. 2/10 X 1
20%

6. B
10% of 300 = 30 and 50% of 20 = 10 so 30 + 10 = 40.

7. C
75%= 75/100 = 3/4

8. D
90% = 90/100 = 9/10

9. B
(Amount Spent) \$420 + \$3000 (Balance) = \$3,420

10. B
9.60/3.2 = 3

11. B
X = 7, so 3x = 3 x 7 = 21, 2x = 2 x 7 = 14, so 21 + 5 - 14 = 26 - 14 = 12

12. A
√121 = 11

13. A
3x = 27, x = 27/3, x = 9

14. A
4y + 24 = 3y + 30, = 4y – 3y + 24 = 30, = y + 24 = 30, = y = 30 – 24, = y = 6

15. D
√144 = 12.

Fraction Tips, Tricks and Shortcuts

When you are writing an exam, time is precious, and anything you can do to answer questions faster, is a real advantage. Here are some ideas, shortcuts, tips and tricks that can speed up answering fraction problems.

Remember that a fraction is just a number which names a portion of something. For instance, instead of having a whole pie, a fraction says you have a part of a pie--such as a half of one or a fourth of one.

Two digits make up a fraction. The digit on top is known as the numerator. The digit on the bottom is known as the denominator. To remember which is which, just remember that “denominator” and “down” both start with a “d.” And the "downstairs" number is the denominator. So for instance, in ½, the numerator is the 1 and the denominator (or "downstairs") number is the 2.

- ☐ It's easy to add two fractions if they have the same denominator. Just add the digits on top and leave the bottom one the same: 1/10 + 6/10 = 7/10.

- ☐ It's the same with subtracting fractions with the same denominator: 7/10 - 6/10 = 1/10.

- ☐ Adding and subtracting fractions with different denominators is more complicated. First, you have to get the problem so that they do have the same denominators. One easiest way to do this is to multiply the denominators: For 2/5 + 1/2 multiply 5 by 2. Now you have a denominator of 10. However, now you have to change the top numbers too. Since you multiplied the 5 in 2/5 by 2, you also multiply the 2 by 2, to get 4. So the first number is now 4/10. Since you multiplied the second number times 5, you also multiply its top number by 5, to get a final fraction of 5/10. Now you can add 5 and 4 together to get a final sum of 9/10.

- ☐ Sometimes you'll be asked to reduce a fraction to its simplest form. This means getting it to where the only common factor of the numerator and denominator is 1. Think of it this way: Numerators and denominators are brothers that must be treated the same. If you do something to one, you must do it to the other, or it's just not fair. For instance, if you divide your numerator by 2, then you should also divide the denominator by the same. Let's take an example: The fraction 2/10 . This is not reduced to its simplest terms because there is a number that will divide evenly into both: the number 2. We want to make it so that the only number that will divide evenly into both is 1. What can we divide into 2 to get 1? The number 2, of course! Now to be "fair," we have to do the same thing to the denominator: Divide 2 into 10 and you get 5. So our new, reduced fraction is 1/5.

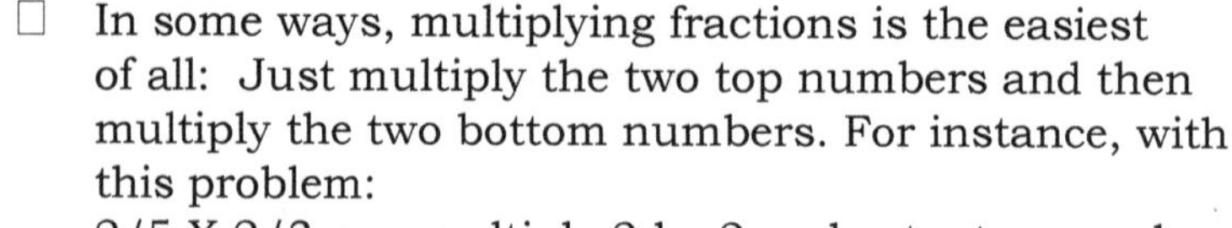

- ☐ In some ways, multiplying fractions is the easiest of all: Just multiply the two top numbers and then multiply the two bottom numbers. For instance, with this problem:
  2/5 X 2/3 you multiply 2 by 2 and get a top number of 4; then multiply 5 by 3 and get a bottom number of 15. Your answer is 4/15.

- ☐ Dividing fractions is more involved, but still not too hard. You once again multiply, but only AFTER you have turned the second fraction upside-down. To divide ⅞ by ½, turn the ½ into 2/1, then multiply the top numbers and multiply the bottom numbers: ⅞ X 2/1 gives us 14 on top and 8 on the bottom.

Converting Fractions to Decimals

There are a couple of ways to become good at converting fractions to decimals. One -- the one that will make you the fastest in basic math skills -- is to learn some basic fraction facts. It's a good idea, if you're good at memory, to memorize the following:

1/100 is "one hundredth," expressed as a decimal, it's .01.

1/50 is "two hundredths," expressed as a decimal, it's .02.

1/25 is "one twenty-fifths" or "four hundredths," expressed as a decimal, it's .04.

1/20 is "one twentieth" or ""five hundredths," expressed as a decimal, it's .05.

1/10 is "one tenth," expressed as a decimal, it's .1.

1/8 is "one eighth," or "one hundred twenty-five thousandths," expressed as a decimal, it's .125.

1/5 is “one fifth,” or “two tenths,” expressed as a decimal, it’s .2.

1/4 is “one fourth” or “twenty-five hundredths,” expressed as a decimal, it’s .25.

1/3 is “one third” or “thirty-three hundredths,” expressed as a decimal, it’s .33.

1/2 is “one half” or “five tenths,” expressed as a decimal, it’s .5.

3/4 is “three fourths,” or “seventy-five hundredths,” expressed as a decimal, it’s .75.

Of course, if you’re no good at memorization, another good technique for converting a fraction to a decimal is to manipulate it so that the fraction’s denominator is 10, 10, 1000, or some other power of 10. Here’s an example: We’ll start with ¾. What is the first number in the 4 “times table” that you can multiply and get a multiple of 10? Can you multiply 4 by something to get 10? No. Can you multiply it by something to get 100? Yes! 4 X 25 is 100. So let’s take that 25 and multiply it by the numerator in our fraction ¾. The numerator is 3, and 3 X 25 is 75. We’ll move the decimal in 75 all the way to the left, and we find that ¾ is .75.

We’ll do another one: 1/5. Again, we want to find a power of 10 that 5 goes into evenly. Will 5 go into 10? Yes! It goes 2 times. So we’ll take that 2 and multiply it by our numerator, 1, and we get 2. We move the decimal in 2 all the way to the left and find that 1/5 is equal to .2.

Converting Fractions to Percent

Working with either fractions or percents can be intimidating enough. But converting from one to the other? That’s a genuine nightmare for those who are not math wizards. But really, it doesn’t have to be that way. Here are two ways to make it easier and faster to convert a fraction to a percent.

- ☐ First, you might remember that a fraction is nothing more than a division problem: you're dividing the bottom number into the top number. So for instance, if we start with a fraction 1/10, we are making a division problem with the 10 on the outside of the bracket and the 1 on the inside. As you remember from your lessons on dividing by decimals, since 10 won't go into 1, you add a decimal and make it 10 into 1.0. 10 into 10 goes 1 time, and since it's behind the decimal, it's .1. And how do we say .1? We say "one tenth," which is exactly what we started with: 1/10. So we have a number we can work with now: .1. When we're dealing with percents, though, we're dealing strictly with hundredths (not tenths). You remember from studying decimals that adding a zero to the right of the number on the right side of the decimal does not change the value. Therefore, we can change .1 into .10 and have the same number--except now it's expressed as hundredths. We have 10 hundredths. That's ten out of 100--which is just another way of saying ten percent (ten per hundred or ten out of 100). In other words .1 = .10 = 10 percent. Remember, if you're changing from a decimal to a percent, get rid of the decimal on the left and replace it with a percent mark on the right: 10%. Let's review those steps again: Divide 10 into 1. Since 10 doesn't go into 1, turn 1 into 1.0. Now divide 10 into 1.0. Since 10 goes into 10 1 time, put it there and add your decimal to make it .1. Since a percent is always "hundredths," let's change .1 into .10. Then remove the decimal on the left and replace with a percent sign on the right. The answer is 10%.

- ☐ If you're doing these conversions on a multiple-choice test, here's an idea that might be even easier and faster. Let's say you have a fraction of 1/8 and you're asked what the percent is. Since we know that "percent" means hundredths, ask yourself what number we can multiply 8 by to get 100. Since there is no number, ask what number gets us close to 100. That number is 12: 8 X 12 = 96. So it gets us a little less than 100. Now, whatever you do to the denominator, you have to do to the numerator. Let's multiply 1 X 12 and we get 12. However, since 96 is a little less than 100, we know that our answer will be a percent a little MORE than 12%. So if your possible answers on the multiple-choice test are these:

a) 8.5% b) 19% c)12.5% d) 25%

then we know the answer is c) 12.5%, because it's a little MORE than the 12 we got in our math problem above.

Another way to look at this, using multiple choice strategy is you know the answer will be "about" 12. Looking at the other choices, they are all either too large or too small and can be eliminated right away.

This was an easy example to demonstrate, so don't be fooled! You probably won't get such an easy question on your exam, but the principle holds just the same. By estimating your answer quickly, you can eliminate choices immediately and save precious exam time.

Decimals Tips, Tricks and Shortcuts

Converting Decimals to Fractions

One of the most important tricks for correctly converting a decimal to a fraction doesn't involve math at all. It's simply to learn to say the decimal correctly. If you say "point one" or "point 25" for .1 and .25, you'll have more trouble getting the conversion correct. But if you know that it's called "one tenth" and "twenty-five hundredths," you're on the way to a correct conversion. That's because, if you know your fractions, you know that "one tenth" looks like this: 1/10. And "twenty-five hundredths" looks like this: 25/100.

Even if you have digits before the decimal, such as 3.4, learning how to say the word will help you with the conversion into a fraction. It's not "three point four," it's "three and four tenths." Knowing this, you know that the fraction which looks like “three and four tenths” is 3 4/10.

Of course, your conversion is not complete until you reduce the fraction to its lowest terms: It’s not 25/100, but 1/4.

Converting Decimals to Percent

Changing a decimal to a percent is easy if you remember one math formula: multiply by 100. For instance, if you start with .45, you change it to a percent by simply multiplying it by 100. You then wind up with 45. Add the % sign to the end and you get 45%.

That seems easy enough, right? Here think of it this way: You just take out the decimal and stick in a percent sign on the opposite sign. In other words, the decimal on the left is replaced by the % on the right.

It doesn’t work that easily if the decimal is in the middle of the number. Let’s use 3.7 for example. Here, take out the decimal in the middle and replace it with a 0 % at the end. So 3.7 converted to decimal is 370%.

Percent Tips, Tricks and Shortcuts

Percent problems are not nearly as scary as they appear, if you remember this neat trick:

Draw a cross as in:

Portion	Percent
Whole	100

In the upper left, write PORTION. In the bottom left write WHOLE. In the top right, write PERCENT and in the bottom right, write 100. Whatever your problem is, you will leave blank the unknown, and fill in the other four parts. For example, let's suppose your problem is: Find 10% of 50. Since we know the 10% part, we put 10 in the percent corner. Since the whole number in our problem is 50, we put that in the corner marked whole. You always put 100 underneath the percent, so we leave it as is, which leaves only the top left corner blank. This is where we will put our answer. Now simply multiply the two corner numbers that are NOT 100. Here, it's 10 X 50. That gives us 500. Now divide this by the remaining corner, or 100, to get a final answer of 5. 5 is the number that goes in the upper-left corner, and is your final solution.
Another hint to remember: Percents are the same as hundredths in decimals. So .45 is the same as 45 hundredths or 45 percent.

Converting Percents to Decimals

Percents are simply a specific type of decimals, so it should be no surprise that converting between the two is actually fairly simple. Here are a few tricks and shortcuts to keep in mind:

- Remember that percent literally means "per 100" or "for every 100." So when you speak of 30% you're saying 30 for every 100 or thc fraction 30/100. In basic math, you learned that fractions that have 10 or 100 as the denominator can easily be turned into a decimal. 30/100 is thirty hundredths, or expressed as a decimal, .30.
- Another way to look at it: To convert a percent to a decimal, simply divide the number by 100. So for instance, if the percent is 47%, divide 47 by 100. The result will be .47. Get rid of the % mark and you're done.
- Remember that the easiest way of dividing by 100 is by moving your decimal two spots to the left.

Converting Percents to Fractions

Converting percents to fractions is easy. After all, a percent is a type of fraction; it tells you what part of 100 that you're talking about. Here are some simple ideas for making the conversion from a percent to a fraction:

- If the percent is a whole number -- say 34% -- then simply write a fraction with 100 as the denominator (the bottom number). Then put the percentage itself on top. So 34% becomes 34/100.
- Now reduce as you would reduce any percent. Here, by dividing 2 into 34 and 2 into 100, you get 17/50.
- If your percent is not a whole number -- say 3.4% --then convert it to a decimal expressed as hundredths. 3.4 is the same as 3.40 (or 3 and forty hundredths). Now ask yourself how you would express "three and forty hundredths" as a fraction. It would, of course, be 3 40/100. Reduce this and it becomes 3 2/5.

How to Answer Basic Math Multiple Choice

Math is the one section where you need to make sure that you understand the processes before you ever tackle it. That's because the time allowed on the math portion is typically so short that there's not much room for error. You have to be fast and accurate. It's imperative that before the test day arrives, you've learned all the main formulas that will be used, and then to create your own problems (and solve them).

On the actual test day, use the "Plug-Check-Check" strategy - here is how it goes.

Read the problem, but not the answers. You'll want to work the problem first and come up with your own answers. If you did the work right, you should find your answer among the choices given.

If you need help with the problem, plug actual numbers into

the variables given. You'll find it easier to work with numbers than it is to work with letters. For instance, if the question asks, "If Y-4 is 2 more than Z, then Y+5 is how much more than Z?" Try selecting a value for Y. Let's take 6. Your question now becomes, "If 6-4 is 2 more than Z, then 6 plus 5 is how much more than Z?" Now your answer should be easier to work with.

Check the choices to see if your answer matches one of those. If so, select it.

If no answer matches the one you got, re-check your math, but this time, use a different method. In math, it's common for there to be more than one way to solve a problem. As a simple example, if you multiplied 12 X 13 and did not get an answer that matches one choice, you might try adding 13 together 12 different times and see if you get a good answer.

Math Multiple Choice Strategy

The two strategies for working with basic math multiple choice are Estimation and Elimination.

Math Strategy 1 - Estimation.

Just like it sounds, try to estimate an approximate answer first. Then look at the choices.

Math Strategy 2 - Elimination.

For every question, no matter what type, eliminating obviously incorrect answers narrows the possible choices. Elimination is probably the most powerful strategy for answering multiple choice.

Here are a few basic math examples of how this works.

Solve 2/3 + 5/12

a. 9/17
b. 3/11
c. 7/12

d. 1 1/12

First estimate the answer. 2/3 is more than half and 5/12 is about half, so the answer is going to be very close to 1.

Next, Eliminate. Choice A is about 1/2 and can be eliminated, choice B is very small, less than 1/2 and can be eliminated. Choice C is close to 1/2 and can be eliminated. Leaving only choice D, which is just over 1.

Work through the solution, a common denominator is needed, a number which both 3 and 12 will divide into.
2/3 = 8/12. So, 8+5/12 = 13/12 = 1 1/12

Choice D is correct.

Solve 4/5 – 2/3

a. 2/2

b. 2/13

c. 1

d. 2/15

You can eliminate choice A, because it is 1 and since both of the numbers are close to one, the difference is going to be very small. You can eliminate choice C for the same reason.

Next, look at the denominators. Since 5 and 3 don't go in to 13, you can eliminate choice B as well.

That leaves choice D.

Checking the answer, the common denominator will be 15. So 12-10/15 = 2/15. Choice D is correct.

Fractions shortcut - Cancelling out.

In any operation with fractions, if the numerator of one fraction has a common multiple with the denominator of the other, you can cancel out. This saves time and simplifies the problem quickly, making it easier to manage.

Solve 2/15 ÷ 4/5

a. 6/65
b. 6/75
c. 5/12
d. 1/6

To divide fractions, we multiply the first fraction with the inverse of the second fraction. Therefore we have 2/15 x 5/4. The numerator of the first fraction, 2, shares a multiple with the denominator of the second fraction, 4, which is 2. These cancel out, which gives, 1/3 x 1/2 = 1/6

Cancelling out solved the questions very quickly, but we can still use multiple choice strategies to answer.

Choice B can be eliminated because 75 is too large a denominator. Choice C can be eliminated because 5 and 15 don't go in to 12.

Choice D is correct.

Decimal Multiple Choice Strategy and Shortcuts.

Multiplying decimals gives a very quick way to estimate and eliminate choices. Anytime that you multiply decimals, it is going to give an answer with the same number of decimal places as the combined operands.

So for example,

2.38 X 1.2 will produce a number with three places of decimal, which is 2.856.

Here are a few examples with step-by-step explanation:

Solve 2.06 x 1.2

a. 24.82
b. 2.482
c. 24.72
d. 2.472

This is a simple question, but even before you start calculating, you can eliminate several choices. When multiplying decimals, there will always be as many numbers behind the decimal place in the answer as the sum of the ones in the initial problem, so choices A and C can be eliminated.

The correct answer is D: 2.06 x 1.2 = 2.472

Solve 20.0 ÷ 2.5

a. 12.05
b. 9.25
c. 8.3
d. 8

First estimate the answer to be around 10, and eliminate choice A. And since it'd also be an even number, you can eliminate choices B and C, leaving only choice D.

The correct answer is D: 20.0 ÷ 2.5 = 8

Order of Operation

Some math calculations contain more than one set of operations. For example, a problem like 3 + (35 - 21) x 2 requires addition, subtraction and multiplication operations. The problem arises from the confusion of which of the operations to perform first. Starting with the wrong operation will give you the wrong answer. To solve this dilemma and to avoid confusion, the Order of Operation rules were set.

Order of operation is a set of mathematical rules designed to be used for calculations that require more than one arithmetic operation. For example, calculation problems that require two or more out of addition, subtraction, multiplication and division, would require that you follow the order of operation to solve.

The order of operation rules are quite simple as explained below.

> **Rule 1:** Start with calculations that are inside brackets or parentheses.
>
> **Rule 2:** Then, solve all multiplications and divisions, from left to right.
>
> **Rule 3:** Finally, solve all additions and subtractions, from left to right.

Example 1

Solve 16 + 5 x 8

Based on the rules above, we would have to start with the multiplication part of the question.
That will give: 16 + 40 = 56

Take note that if the rule was not followed and addition was done first, the answer gotten would be different and wrong.

16 + 5 x 8
21 x 8 = 168 (wrong answer)

Example 2

3 +(35 - 21) x 2

Based on the rules of the order of operation, we have to solve the problem in the bracket or parenthesis first. Then we do the multiplication, before doing the addition.

3 + (35 - 21) x 2

3 + (14) x 3
3 + 42
= 45

Logic

THIS SECTION CONTAINS A SELF-ASSESSMENT AND LOGIC TUTORIAL. The tutorials are designed to familiarize general principles and the self-assessment contains general questions similar to the logic questions likely to be on the RCMP Entrance Test, but are not intended to be identical to the exam questions. The tutorials are not designed to be a complete reading course, and it is assumed that students have some familiarity with logic questions. If you do not understand parts of the tutorial, or find the tutorial difficult, it is recommended that you seek out additional instruction.

Tour of the RCMP Test Logic

The RCMP logic section has 20 questions. Below is a detailed list of the types of reading questions that generally appear on the RCMP test.

- Ordering information in a logical sequence
- Map reading
- Solving problems
- Identifying patterns in data

The questions below are not the same as you will find on the RCMP test- that would be too easy! And nobody knows what the questions will be and they change all the time. Mostly the changes consist of substituting new questions for old, but the changes can be new question formats or styles, changes to the number of questions in each section, changes to the time limits for each section and combining sections. Below are general logic questions that cover the same areas and are intended for skill practice. While the format and exact wording of the questions may differ slightly, and change from year to year, if you can answer the questions below, you will have no problem with the logic section of the RCMP test.

Logic Self-Assessment

The purpose of the self-assessment is:

- Identify your strengths and weaknesses.
- Develop your personalized study plan (above)
- Get accustomed to the RCMP Entrance test format
- Extra practice – the self-assessments are almost a full 3rd practice test!
- Provide a baseline score for preparing your study schedule.

Since this is a Self-assessment, and depending on how confident you are with logic and problem solving, timing is optional. The RCMP has 20 logic questions. The self-assessment has 10 questions, so allow about 10 minutes to complete.

Once complete, use the table below to assess your understanding of the content, and prepare your study schedule described in chapter 1.

80% - 100%	Excellent – you have mastered the content
60 – 79%	Good. You have a working knowledge. Even though you can just pass this section, you may want to review the tutorials and do some extra practice to see if you can improve your mark.
40% - 59%	Below Average. You do not understand verbal skills problems. Review the tutorials, and retake this quiz again in a few days, before proceeding to the Practice Test Questions.
Less than 40%	Poor. You have a very limited understanding of verbal skills problems. Please review the tutorials, and retake this quiz again in a few days, before proceeding to the Practice Test Questions.

Directions: Find the sentence that is true according to the given information.

5. Krizzia loves reading books. Nea enjoys playing with her dolls. Krizzia and Nea are cousins.

a. Krizzia likes to play with Nea.

b. Nea finds reading boring.

c. Krizzia and Nea are blood related

d. Nea and Krizzia are best friends.

6. The village is found in a coastal area. Many fishermen go out to sea everyday. They go home late in the afternoon.

a. Fishing is the means of living of the villagers.

b. Many fishermen hate fishing.

c. Fishermen go out to sea especially in the evening.

d. The village attracts tourists.

Question 7 is based on the following information.

7. Five billboards appear on a highway. They are numbered from 1 to 5, starting at 1, and proceeding up to 5 as you drive by.

a. The first billboard is for Lasik eye surgery.

b. A Vietnamese restaurant is 2nd.

c. There are 3 billboards between the Lasik Eye surgery billboard and the McDonalds' Billboard.

d. There is one billboard before the Life Insurance billboard.

What position is the Wells Fargo Billboard?

a. Second
b. Third
c. Fourth
d. Cannot be determined.

8. Place the following four sentences in logical order.

1. Interview suspect who claims he isn't married
2. Called to domestic dispute
3. Suspect flees on foot and is apprehended
4. Computer search reveals a man matching the suspects description is the husband of the woman making the complaint

a. 2, 3, 1, 4
b. 4, 2, 3, 1
c. 3, 2, 1, 4
d. The order is correct

You are interviewing a woman who has been assaulted walking home from the bus stop. You ask her to re-trace her steps from the bus stop.

She got off the bus on Victoria Ave. and walked to Birch st., where she turned right. She walked along Birch St. and turned right on Elm St. She first notice she was being followed on Elm. She continued walking on Elm and turned left on Maple St. Her assailant tried to grab her purse on Maple St. She escaped and ran down Maple, turning left on Spruce, where she ran north to her house.

9. What direction was she travelling on Elm?

a. North
b. South
c. East
d. West

10. What direction was she travelling when she noticed she was attacked?

a. North
b. South
c. East
d. West

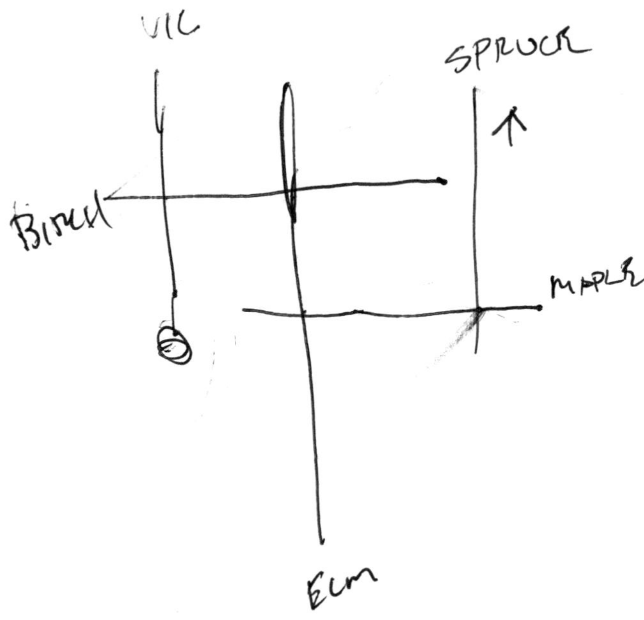

Answer Key

Section I – Number Series

1. D
The numbers double each time.

2. A
Each number is the sum of the previous two numbers.

3. C
The numbers decrease by 5 each time.

4. C
The numbers are primes (divisible only by 1 and themselves).

5. C
The only certain thing is Krizzia and Nea are related to each other.

6. A
The only certain thing is the villagers rely on fishing to earn money since they live near the ocean.

7. B
Lasik is #1. The Vietnamese restaurant is #2, and there is 1 before the Life Insurance, so Life Insurance must be 4th. There are 3 billboards between Lasik and McDonalds, so Lasik and McDonalds must be first and last. The only position left for Wells Fargo is #3.

1 Lasik Eye Surgery

2 - Vietnamese Restaurant

3 -

4 - Life Insurance

5 - McDonalds

8. A
2, 3, 1, 4

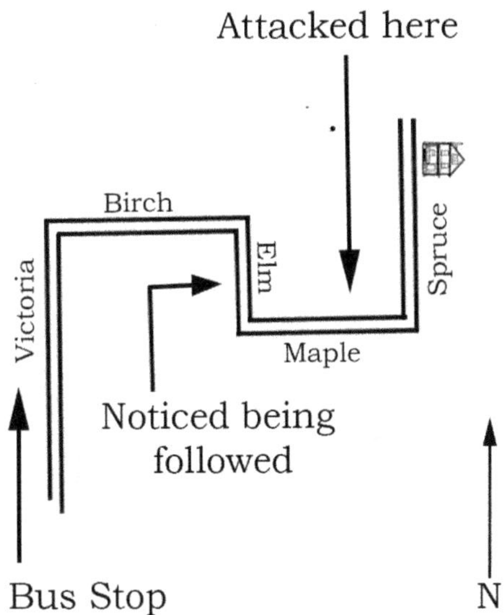

9. B
She was travelling South on Elm.

10. C
She was travelling East on Maple when she was attacked.

Number Series Tutorial

Number series questions appear on most High School exams. An example is:
Consider the following series: 26, 21, 0, 11, 6. What is the missing number?

a. 27
b. 23
c. 16
d. 29

Looking carefully at the sequence, we can see right away that each number is 5 less than the previous number, so the missing number is 16.

We can re-write this sequence in mathematical notation as, a_1, a_2, a_3, ... an, where n is an integer and an is called its nth term. And we can write the sequence in the form of a formula, where an integer is substituted in the place of the variable in the formula and the terms are obtained.

For example, let us consider the sequence 5,10,15,20,...

- Here, $a_n = 5n$. The formula $a_n = 5n$.
- The nth term of a sequence can be found by plugging n in the explicit formula for the sequence. So for example if we wanted to find the 100th number in this sequence, we would substitute n = 100 in the formula and get 500.

Type of Number Sequence problems

1. Simple addition or subtraction – each number in the sequence is obtained by adding a number to the previous number.

For example, 2, 5, 8, 11, 14

Each number in the sequence is obtained by adding 3 to the previous number, which we could write as, $a_{n+1} = a_n + 3$.

2. Simple multiplication - each number in the sequence is obtained by multiplying the previous number by a whole number or fraction.

For example, 3, 6, 18, 54

Or,

20, 10, 5, 2.5

Each number in the first sequence is obtained by multiplying the previous number by 3, which we could write as, $a_{n+1} = a_n X 3$.

In the second example, each number in the series is the previous number divided by 2, or multiplied by 1/2, or $a_{n+1} = a_n X 1/2$.

3. Prime Numbers – each number in the sequence is a prime number.

For example,

23, ..., 31, 37

Answer: 29

4. Operations on the previous two numbers. For example,

8, 14, 22, 36, 58

Here the sequence is created by adding the previous 2 numbers.

5. Exponents. The number sequence is created by each number squared or cubed.

For example,

3, 9, 81, 6561, where each number is squared.

6. Combining Sequences

2, 7, 13, 20, 28, 37

Here the sequence starts with 2, and each element is added to another sequence starting with 5. So, 2 + 5 = 7, 7 + 6 = 13, 13 + 7 = 20 and so on.

A variation is a sequence with a repeating element. For example,

1, 2, 3, 5, 7, 9, 12, 15

Here the sequence is, for each n, +1, +1, +1, +2, +2, +2, +3, +3,

7. Fractions

For example,

16/4, 4/2, 2/2, ½, 0

Fractions are often meant to confuse. If fractions don't have an obvious relationship, reduce them to lowest terms or to whole numbers. Reducing these to whole numbers, gives,

4, 2, 1, ½

Right away, we can see the numbers are half the previous number, so the next in the series is 1/4.

In this example, the answer is a fraction; however, you may have to reduce fractions to see the relation, and then convert back to get the answer in the correct form.

Strategy for Answering Number Series Questions

Answering number series questions is a skill of recognizing patterns, and the best way to improve is to familiarize yourself with the different types, and to practice.

Here is a quick method that will help you answer number series.

For example:

2, 5, 6, 7, 8, ...

Step 1 – glance at the series quickly and see if you can spot the pattern right away.

Step 2 – Start analyzing.

Take the different between the first 2 numbers and the different between the second 2 numbers.

2, (+3) 5, (+1) 6, (+1) 7, (+1) 8,

No clear pattern with a simple analysis. There is no addition, subtraction, multiplication, division, fractional or exponent relationship.

The relation must be a higher order or a second series.

Next look at the relation between the 1st number and the 2nd and the 1st and the 3rd. We see that,
1st + 3 = 5, 1st + 4 = 6. That's it! The number 2 is added to the sequence, 3, 4, 5, 6, so the next number will be 2 + 7 = 9.

Practice Test Questions Set 1

THE QUESTIONS BELOW ARE NOT THE SAME AS YOU WILL FIND ON THE RCMP ENTRANCE TEST- THAT WOULD BE TOO EASY! And nobody knows what the questions will be and they change all the time. Below are general questions that cover the same subject areas as the RCMP Entrance Test. So, while the format and exact wording of the questions may differ slightly, and change from year to year, if you can answer the questions below, you will have no problem with the RCMP Entrance Test.

For the best results, take these practice test questions as if it were the real exam. Set aside time when you will not be disturbed, and a location that is quiet and free of distractions. Read the instructions carefully, read each question carefully, and answer to the best of your ability.

Use the bubble answer sheets provided. When you have completed the practice questions, check your answer against the Answer Key and read the explanation provided.

Do not attempt more than one set of practice test questions in one day. After completing the first practice test, wait two or three days before attempting the second set of questions.

Part I - Reading Comprehension

Questions 1 – 4 refer to the following passage.

Passage 1 - Infectious Disease

An infectious disease is a clinically evident illness resulting from the presence of pathogenic agents, such as viruses, bacteria, fungi, protozoa, multi-cellular parasites, and unusual proteins known as prions. Infectious pathologies are also called communicable diseases or transmissible diseases, due to their potential of transmission from one person or species to another by a replicating agent (as opposed to a toxin).

Transmission of an infectious disease can occur in many different ways. Physical contact, liquids, food, body fluids, contaminated objects, and airborne inhalation can all transmit infecting agents.

Transmissible diseases that occur through contact with an ill person, or objects touched by them, are especially infective, and are sometimes called contagious diseases. Communicable diseases that require a more specialized route of infection, such as through blood or needle transmission, or sexual transmission, are usually not regarded as contagious.

The term infectivity describes the ability of an organism to enter, survive and multiply in the host, while the infectiousness of a disease shows the comparative ease with which the disease is transmitted. An infection however, is not synonymous with an infectious disease, as an infection may not cause important clinical symptoms. [3]

1. What can we infer from the first paragraph in this passage?

a. Sickness from a toxin can be easily transmitted from one person to another.

b. Sickness from an infectious disease can be easily transmitted from one person to another.

c. Few sicknesses are transmitted from one person to another.

d. Infectious diseases are easily treated.

2. What are two other names for infections' pathologies?

a. Communicable diseases or transmissible diseases

b. Communicable diseases or terminal diseases

c. Transmissible diseases or preventable diseases

d. Communicative diseases or unstable diseases

3. What does infectivity describe?

a. The inability of an organism to multiply in the host.

b. The inability of an organism to reproduce.

c. The ability of an organism to enter, survive and multiply in the host.

d. The ability of an organism to reproduce in the host.

4. How do we know an infection is not synonymous with an infectious disease?

a. Because an infectious disease destroys infections with enough time.

b. Because an infection may not cause important clinical symptoms or impair host function.

c. We do not. The two are synonymous.

d. Because an infection is too fatal to be an infectious disease.

Questions 5 – 8 refer to the following passage.

Passage 2 - Virus

A virus (from the Latin virus meaning toxin or poison) is a small infectious agent that can replicate only inside the living cells of other organisms. Most viruses are too small to be seen directly with a microscope. Viruses infect all types of organisms, from animals and plants to bacteria and single-celled organisms.

Unlike prions and viroids, viruses consist of two or three parts: all viruses have genes made from either DNA or RNA, all have a protein coat that protects these genes, and some have an envelope of fat that surrounds them when they are outside a cell. (Viroids do not have a protein coat and prions contain no RNA or DNA.) Viruses vary from simple to very complex structures. Most viruses are about one hundred times smaller than an average bacterium. The origins of viruses in the evolutionary history of life are unclear: some may have evolved from plasmids—pieces of DNA that can move between cells—while others may have evolved from bacteria.

Viruses spread in many ways; plant viruses are often transmitted from plant to plant by insects that feed on sap, such as aphids, while animal viruses can be carried by blood-sucking insects. These disease-bearing organisms are known as vectors. Influenza viruses are spread by coughing and sneezing. HIV is one of several viruses transmitted through sexual contact and by exposure to infected blood. Viruses can infect only a limited range of host cells called the "host range." This can be broad, as a virus is capable of infecting many species or narrow. [4]

5. What can we infer from the first paragraph in this selection?

a. A virus is the same as bacterium.

b. A person with excellent vision can see a virus with the naked eye.

c. A virus cannot be seen with the naked eye.

d. Not all viruses are dangerous.

6. What types of organisms do viruses infect?

a. Only plants and humans

b. Only animals and humans

c. Only disease-prone humans

d. All types of organisms

7. How many parts do prions and viroids consist of?

a. Two

b. Three

c. Either less than two or more than three

d. Less than two

8. What is one common virus spread by coughing and sneezing?

a. AIDS

b. Influenza

c. Herpes

d. Tuberculosis

Questions 9 – 11 refer to the following passage.

Passage 3 – Thunderstorms

The first stage of a thunderstorm is the cumulus stage, or developing stage. In this stage, masses of moisture are lifted upwards into the atmosphere. The trigger for this lift can be insulation heating the ground producing thermals, areas where two winds converge, forcing air upwards, or, where winds blow over terrain of increasing elevation. Moisture in the air rapidly cools into liquid drops of water, which appears as cumulus clouds.

As the water vapour condenses into liquid, latent heat is released which warms the air, causing it to become less dense than the surrounding dry air. The warm air rises in an updraft through the process of convection (hence the term convective precipitation). This creates a low-pressure zone beneath the forming thunderstorm. In a typical thunderstorm, about 5×10^8 kg of water vapour is lifted, and the quantity of energy released when this condenses is about equal to the energy used by a city of 100,000 in a month. [5]

9. The cumulus stage of a thunderstorm is the

a. The last stage of the storm.

b. The middle stage of the storm formation.

c. The beginning of the thunderstorm.

d. The period after the thunderstorm has ended.

10. One of the ways the air is warmed is

a. Air moving downwards, which creates a high-pressure zone.

b. Air cooling and becoming less dense, causing it to rise.

c. Moisture moving downward toward the earth.

d. Heat created by water vapour condensing into liquid.

11. Identify the correct sequence of events

a. Warm air rises, water droplets condense, creating more heat, and the air rises further.

b. Warm air rises and cools, water droplets condense, causing low pressure.

c. Warm air rises and collects water vapour, the water vapour condenses as the air rises, which creates heat, and causes the air to rise further.

d. None of the above.

Questions 12 – 15 refer to the following passage.

Passage 4 – US Weather Service

The United States National Weather Service classifies thunderstorms as severe when they reach a predetermined level. Usually, this means the storm is strong enough to inflict wind or hail damage. In most of the United States, a storm is considered severe if winds reach over 50 knots (58 mph or 93 km/h), hail is ¾ inch (2 cm) diameter or larger, or if meteorologists report funnel clouds or tornadoes. In the Central Region of the United States National Weather Service, the hail threshold for a severe thunderstorm is 1 inch (2.5 cm) in diameter. Though a funnel cloud or tornado shows the presence of a severe thunderstorm, the various meteorological agencies would issue a tornado warning rather than a severe thunderstorm warning.

Meteorologists in Canada define a severe thunderstorm as either having tornadoes, wind gusts of 90 km/h or greater, hail 2 centimeters in diameter or greater, rainfall more than 50 millimeters in 1 hour, or 75 millimeters in 3 hours.

Severe thunderstorms can develop from any type of thunderstorm. [6]

12. What is the purpose of this passage?

a. Explaining when a thunderstorm turns into a tornado.

b. Explaining who issues storm warnings, and when these warnings should be issued.

c. Explaining when meteorologists consider a thunderstorm severe.

d. None of the above.

13. It is possible to infer from this passage that

a. Different areas and countries have different criteria for determining a severe storm.

b. Thunderstorms can include lightning and tornadoes, as well as violent winds and large hail.

c. If someone spots both a thunderstorm and a tornado, meteorological agencies will immediately issue a severe storm warning.

d. Canada has a different alert system for severe storms, with criteria that are far less.

14. What would the Central Region of the United States National Weather Service do if hail was 2.7 cm in diameter?

a. Not issue a severe thunderstorm warning.

b. Issue a tornado warning.

c. Issue a severe thunderstorm warning.

d. Sleet must also accompany the hail before the Weather Service will issue a storm warning.

15. When would a tornado warning be issued instead of a thunderstorm warning?

a. A tornado warning would be issued when there is a funnel cloud or a tornado.

b. A tornado warning would be issued when there is a funnel cloud.

c. A tornado warning is issued when there is a severe thunderstorm.

d. None of the above.

Questions 16 – 19 refer to the following passage.

Passage 5 - If You Have Allergies, You're Not Alone

People who experience allergies might joke that their immune systems have let them down or are seriously lacking. Truthfully though, people who experience allergic reactions or allergy symptoms during certain times of the year have heightened immune systems that are, "better" than those of people who have perfectly healthy but less militant immune systems.
Still, when a person has an allergic reaction, they are having an adverse reaction to a substance that is considered normal to most people. Mild allergic reactions usually have symptoms like itching, runny nose, red eyes, or bumps or discoloration of the skin. More serious allergic reactions, such as those to animal and insect poisons or certain foods, may result in the closing of the throat, swelling of the eyes, low blood pressure, inability to breathe, and can even be fatal.

Different treatments help different allergies, and which one a person uses depends on the nature and severity of the allergy. It is recommended to patients with severe allergies to take extra precautions, such as carrying an EpiPen, which treats anaphylactic shock and may prevent death, always in order for the remedy to be readily available and more effective. When an allergy is not so severe, treatments may be used just relieve a person of uncomfortable symptoms. Over the counter allergy medicines treat milder symptoms, and can be bought at any grocery store and used in moderation to help people with allergies live normally.

There are many tests available to assess whether a person has allergies or what they may be allergic to, and advances in these tests and the medicine used to treat patients continues to improve. Despite this fact, allergies still affect many people throughout the year or even every day. Medicines used to treat allergies have side effects of their own, and it is difficult to bring the body into balance with the use of medicine. Regardless, many of those who live with allergies are grateful for what is available and find it useful in maintaining their lifestyles.

16. According to this passage, it can be understood that the word "militant" belongs in a group with the words:

a. sickly, ailing, faint
b. strength, power, vigor
c. active, fighting, warring
d. worn, tired, breaking down

17. The author says that "medicines used to treat allergies have side effects of their own" to

a. point out that doctors aren't very good at diagnosing and treating allergies.

b. argue that because of the large number of people with allergies, a cure will never be found.

c. explain that allergy medicines aren't cures and some compromise must be made.

d. argue that more wholesome remedies should be researched and medicines banned.

18. It can be inferred that ______ recommend that some people with allergies carry medicine with them.

a. the author

b. doctors

c. the makers of EpiPen

d. people with allergies

19. The author has written this passage to

a. inform readers on symptoms of allergies so people with allergies can get help.

b. persuade readers to be proud of having allergies.

c. inform readers on different remedies so people with allergies receive the right help.

d. describe different types of allergies, their symptoms, and their remedies.

Question 20 refers to the following passage.

Passage 6 - Clouds

A cloud is a visible mass of droplets or frozen crystals floating in the atmosphere above the surface of the Earth or other planetary bodies. Another type of cloud is a mass of material in space, attracted by gravity, called interstellar clouds and nebulae. The branch of meteorology which studies clouds is called nephrology. When we are speaking of Earth clouds, water vapor is usually the condensing substance, which forms small droplets or ice crystal. These crystals are typically 0.01 mm in diameter. Dense, deep clouds reflect most light, so they appear white, at least from the top. Cloud droplets scatter light very efficiently, so the farther into a cloud light travels, the weaker it gets. This accounts for the gray or dark appearance at the base of large clouds. Thin clouds may appear to have acquired the color of their environment or background. [7]

20. The main idea of this passage is

a. Condensation occurs in clouds, having an intense effect on the weather on the surface of the earth.

b. Atmospheric gases are responsible for the gray color of clouds just before a severe storm happens.

c. A cloud is a visible mass of droplets or frozen crystals floating in the atmosphere above the surface of the Earth or other planetary body.

d. Clouds reflect light in varying amounts and degrees, depending on the size and concentration of the water droplets.

Part II - Observation, Professional Judgement, Recognition and Identification.

Section I - Observation

Directions: You have five minutes to memorize the following information. Do not write anything down. Questions follow on page 163.

Name: William Jackson

Description: 5’11” Caucasian male. Brown hair with receding hairline. Slight build. No identifying marks.

Wanted for: Armed Robbery

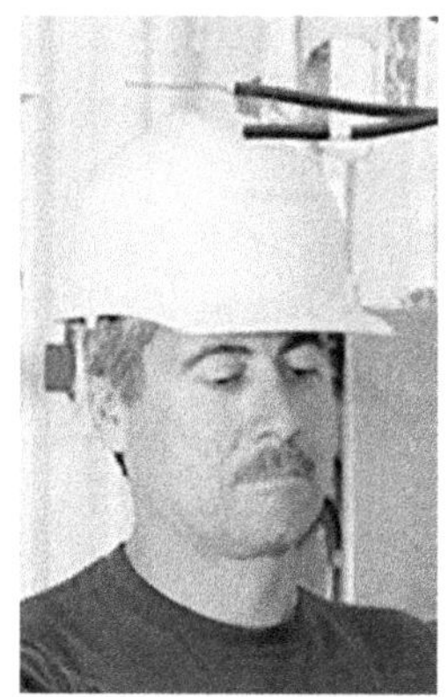

Name: Kenneth Walker

Description: 5 ft. Caucasian male with heavy build. Small scar on right forehead.

Wanted for: Armed robbery

Make: Porche Carrera

Color: White

License: Manitoba APT 936

Wanted for: Dangerous Driving

Make: Smart Car

Color: White

License: New Brunswick CPV 439

Wanted for: Criminal Harassment

Name: Steven Hermandez

Description: 6 ft Latino male with tattoos on both arms and chest.

Wanted For: Theft of motor vehicle

Name: Linda Moore

Description: 5' 4" Caucasian female, blonde hair, brown eyes, tattoos on left forearm

Wanted For: Shoplifting

Make: Volkwagen Passat

Color: White

License: British Columbia AG5 26C

Wanted for: Sexual Assault

Make: Volkwagen Beetle

Color: Yellow

License: AG5 26C

Wanted for: Sexual Assault

Section II - Professional Judgement

Scenario I

You and your partner arrive on a domestic scene where an enraged and possibly drunk or high man is destroying the furniture in a house. His wife or girlfriend is crying nearby.

1. What should you do first?

a. Subdue the man and then report to dispatch
b. Report to dispatch and call for backup
c. Make sure the wife is OK
d. Check the wife first, then subdue the man

You have confirmed the girlfriend is OK and subdued and placed the man under arrest. He has calmed down. You and your partner are preparing to take the man to the station. He begs you to release him saying it was all a big misunderstanding.

2. What should you do now?

a. Release the man if he agrees to appear in court.

b. Take the man to the station.

c. Discuss what to do with your partner.

d. Ask dispatch what to do.

Scenario II

You attend a fight in a parking lot near a popular nightclub that has just closed. You and your partner find one man with a bloody nose and looking poorly, and another man who appears to be fine. There is a crowd watching the fight.

3. What should you do?

a. Check the injured man, keeping the men separate.

b. Arrest both men

c. Arrest both men and interview them separately.

d. Check the injured man, interview both men separately.

Scenario III

4. You have just arrested a man for breaking and entering. You apprehended the suspect inside a residence with broken windows. The man tells you he will give you the name of 2 other people who recently robbed a bank in your patrol area if you let him go.

What should you do?

a. Take down the information and let him go.

b. Take down the information and continue with the arrest and processing.

c. Tell him he will have to give you information about 2 or more crimes before you can let him go

d. Call dispatch for advice.

Scenario IV

5. You have pulled over a vehicle for dangerous driving and arrested the driver. The driver of the vehicle has agreed to accompany you to the station. The driver has requested he drive his own vehicle behind yours.

What should you do?

a. You determine the driver has not been drinking and appears calm, so you allow the driver to follow you to the station.

b. Refuse his request and ask dispatch to call a tow truck.

c. Question the driver more before allowing him to drive back

d. Allow the suspect to drive his own car back with some restrictions.

Scenario V

6. You attend a call to a beach party. Nearby some cars have been vandalized. It is not clear if the people at the beach party are responsible or not, and they deny vandalizing the cars. There are 8 or 10 people at the beach party and they appear peaceful.

What should you do?

a. Call for backup before approaching the beach party.

b. Approach the beach party and ask if they know about the vandalized cars.

c. Arrest everyone at the beach party.

d. Take the names of everyone at the party.

7. Backup has arrived and you approach the beach party with 2 other officers. You are the senior officer at the scene.

What is your next step?

a. Arrest everyone at the party

b. Question everyone at the party about the vandalized cars

c. Accuse everyone at the party of vandalizing the cars to see their reaction

d. Examine the vandalized cars with the other officers.

Scenario VI

8. You have pulled over a car for speeding and are about to write up a ticket. The driver tells you he knows the mayor and the chief of police and will get you fired if you give him a ticket. He asked for your name and badge number.

What should you do?

a. Refuse to give your name or badge.

b. Give the driver a warning instead of a ticket

c. Let the driver go

d. Give your name and badge number and give him a ticket.

Scenario VII

You have attended a domestic violence call. The woman has clearly been beaten by the man, and when you enter the house, the man is breaking china and furniture.

9. What should you do first?

a. Stop the man from further property damage.
b. Attend the woman's injuries
c. Call for backup
d. Check the house for other people or children.

Scenario VIII

You are called to a robbery at a jewelry store. You arrive and the owner of the store is unconscious and the a male is exiting the store by the front door as you enter the back. The male robbery suspect is carrying a bag, which may contain jewelry from the store.

10. What should you do?

a. Chase the robbery suspect.
b. Check the unconscious owner
c. Assess what has been stolen
d. Call for backup

Section III - Recognition and Identification

11. Choose the person that matches the suspect below.

a.

b.

c.

d.

12. Choose the person that matches the suspect below.

a.

b.

c.

d.

13. Choose the person that matches the suspect below.

a. 

b. 

c. 

d. 

Section I - Observation Questions

Directions: Answer questions 14 - 20 based on the information given on page 151.

14. What identifying marks does Kenneth Walker have?

a. Scar on forehead
b. Tattoo on chest
c. Tattoo on right arm
d. No identifying marks

15. What is Kenneth Walker wanted for?

a. Dangerous Driving
b. Armed Robbery
c. Fraud
d. Criminal Harassment

16. Which car is wanted for Dangerous Driving?

a. Porche Carrera
b. Smart Car
c. Volkwagen Passat
d. None of the above.

17. What Province is the Smart Car from?

a. British Columbia
b. New Brunswick
c. Alberta
d. Ontario

18. What is Steven Hermandez wanted for?

a. Theft of motor vehicle

b. Fraud

c. Armed Robbery

d. Criminal Harassement

19. What identifying marks does Linda Moore have?

a. No identifying marks

b. Scar on forehead

c. Tattoos on forearm

d. Scar on upper lip

20. What color is the Volkswagen Beetle?

a. White

b. Yellow

c. Red

d. Blue

Part III – Composition

1. Choose a verb that means fearless or invulnerable to intimidation and fear.

a. Feeble

b. Strongest

c. Dauntless

d. Super

2. Choose a word that means the same as the underlined word.

I see the differences when they are placed side-by-side and <u>juxtaposed.</u>

a. Compared

b. Eliminated

c. Overturned

d. Exonerated

3. Choose the best definition of regicide.

a. v. To endow or furnish with requisite ability, character, knowledge and skill

b. n. killing of a king

c. adj. Disposed to seize by violence or by unlawful or greedy methods

d. v. To refresh after labor

4. Choose the best definition of pernicious.

a. Deadly

b. Infectious

c. Common

d. Rare

5. Fill in the blank.

After she received her influenza vaccination, Nan thought that she was _______ to the common cold.

a. Immune

b. Susceptible

c. Vulnerable

d. At risk

6. Choose a word that means the same as the underlined word.

She performed the gymnastics and stretches so well! I have never seen anyone so nimble.

a. Awkward

b. Agile

c. Quick

d. Taut

7. Choose a word that means the same as the underlined word.

Are there any more queries? We have already had so many questions today.

a. Questions

b. Commands

c. Obfuscations

d. Paradoxes

8. Choose a verb that means to remove a leader or high official from position.

a. Sack

b. Suspend

c. Depose

d. Dropped

9. Choose the best definition of pedestrian.

a. Rare

b. Often

c. Walking or Running

d. Commonplace

10. Choose the best definition of petulant.

a. Patient
b. Childish
c. Impatient
d. Mature

11. Choose the correct spelling.

a. Humoros
b. Humouros
c. Humorous
d. Humorus

12. Choose the correct spelling.

a. Knowlege
b. Knowledge
c. Knowlegde
d. Knowlledge

13. Choose the correct spelling.

a. Camaraderie
b. Camaredere
c. Camaradere
d. Cameraderie

14. Choose the correct spelling.

a. Mathematics
b. Mathmatics
c. Matematics
d. Mathamatics

15. Choose the correct spelling.

a. Conscentious
b. Conscientios
c. Conscientious
d. Consceintious

16. Choose the correct spelling.

a. Leisuire
b. Lesure
c. Lesure
d. Leisure

17. Choose the correct spelling.

a. Pigeone
b. Pigoen
c. Pigeon
d. Pidgeon

18. Choose the correct spelling.

a. Odyessy
b. Odeyssey
c. Odysey
d. Odyssey

19. Choose the correct spelling.

a. Sacreligious
b. Sacriligious
c. Sacrilegious
d. Sacrilegous

20. Choose the correct spelling.

a. Accommodate
b. Accomodate
c. Acommodate
d. Accommodaite

21. Choose the sentence with the correct capitalization.

a. My favorite Dylan song is blowin' in the wind.
b. My favorite dylan song is Blowin' in the Wind.
c. My favorite Dylan song is Blowin' in the Wind.
d. None of the above.

22. Choose the sentence with the correct capitalization.

a. My latest novel, Danger on the Rhine will be published next year.

b. My latest novel, danger on the Rhine will be published next year.

c. My latest novel, danger on the rhine will be published next year.

d. None of the above.

23. Choose the sentence with the correct usage.

a. The Chinese live in one of the world's most populous nations, while a citizen of Bermuda lives in one of the least populous.

b. The Chinese lives in one of the world's most populous nations, while a citizen of Bermuda live in one of the least populous.

c. The Chinese live in one of the world's most populous nations, while a citizen of Bermuda live in one of the least populous.

d. The Chinese lives in one of the world's most populous nations, while a citizen of Bermuda lives in one of the least populous.

24. Choose the sentence with the correct usage.

a. Disease is highly prevalent in poorer nations; the most dominant disease is malaria.

b. Disease are highly prevalent in poorer nations; the most dominant disease is malaria.

c. Disease is highly prevalent in poorer nations; the most dominant disease are malaria.

d. Disease are highly prevalent in poorer nations; the most dominant disease are malaria.

25. Choose the sentence with the correct usage.

a. Although I would prefer to have dog, I actually own a cat.

b. Although I would prefer to have a dog, I actually own cat.

c. Although I would prefer to have a dog, I actually own a cat.

d. Although I would prefer to have dog, I actually own cat.

36. Choose the sentence with the correct usage.

a. The volunteers brought groceries and toys to the homeless shelter; the latter were given to the staff, while the former were given directly to the children.

b. The volunteers brought groceries and toys to the homeless shelter; the former was given to the staff, while the latter was given directly to the children.

c. The volunteers brought groceries and toys to the homeless shelter; the groceries were given to the staff, while the former was given directly to the children.

d. The volunteers brought groceries and toys to the homeless shelter; the latter was given to the staff, while the groceries were given directly to the children.

27. Choose the sentence with the correct grammar.

a. His doctor suggested that he eat less snacks and do fewer lounging on the couch.

b. His doctor suggested that he eat fewer snacks and do less lounging on the couch.

c. His doctor suggested that he eat less snacks and do less lounging on the couch.

d. His doctor suggested that he eat fewer snacks and do fewer lounging on the couch.

28. Choose the sentence with the correct grammar.

a. However, I believe that he didn't really try that hard.

b. However I believe that he didn't really try that hard.

c. However; I believe that he didn't really try that hard.

d. However: I believe that he didn't really try that hard.

29. Choose the sentence with the correct grammar.

a. There was however, very little difference between the two.

b. There was, however very little difference between the two.

c. There was; however, very little difference between the two.

d. There was, however, very little difference between the two.

30. Choose the sentence with the correct grammar.

a. Don would never have thought of that book, but you could have reminded him.

b. Don would never of thought of that book, but you could have reminded him.

c. Don would never have thought of that book, but you could of have reminded him.

d. Don would never of thought of that book, but you could of reminded him.

Part IV – Math

1. What is 1/3 of 3/4?

a. 1/4
b. 1/3
c. 2/3
d. 3/4

2. What fraction of $1500 is $75?

a. 1/14
b. 3/5
c. 7/10
d. 1/20

3. 3.14 + 2.73 + 23.7 =

a. 28.57
b. 30.57
c. 29.56
d. 29.57

4. A woman spent 15% of her income on an item and ends with $120. What percentage of her income is left?

a. 12%
b. 85%
c. 75%
d. 95%

5. A mother is making spaghetti for her son. The recipe that she's using says that for 500 grams of spaghetti, she should add 0.75 grams of salt. However, the mom just wants 125 grams of spaghetti. Based on this information, how much salt should she use?

a. 0.38 grams
b. 0.75 grams
c. 0.19 grams
d. 0.25 grams

6. A pet store sold $19,304.56 worth of merchandise in June. If the cost of products sold was $5,284.34, employees were paid $8,384.76, and rent was $2,920.00, how much profit did the store make in June?

a. $5,635.46
b. $2,714.46
c. $14,020.22
d. $10,019.80

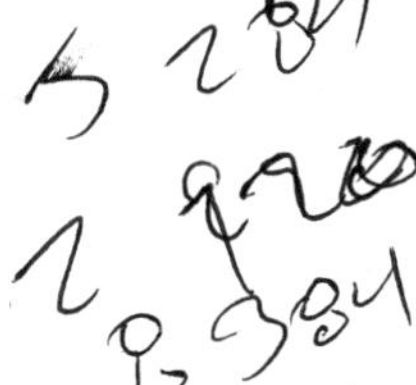

7. At the beginning of 2009, Madalyn invested $5,000 in a savings account. The account pays 4% interest per year. At the end of the year, after the interest was awarded, how much did Madalyn have in the account?

a. $5,200
b. $5,020
c. $5,110
d. $7,000

8. If 144 students need to go on a trip and the buses each carry 36 students, how many buses are needed?

a. 6
b. 5
c. 4
d. 3

9. If a square if five feet tall, what is its area?

a. 5 square feet
b. 10 square feet
c. 20 square feet
d. 25 square feet

10. With a purely random guess, what are the chances of correctly guessing the month in which a person was born?

a. 1 : 3
b. 1 : 6
c. 1 : 4
d. 1 : 12

11. John is a barber and receives 40% of the amount paid by each of his customers. John gets all tips paid to him. If a man pays $8.50 for a haircut and pays a tip of $1.30, how much money goes to John?

a. $3.92
b. $4.70
c. $5.30
d. $6.40

12. Susan was surprised to find she had two more quarters than she believed she had in her purse. If quarters are the only coins, and the total is $8.75, how many quarters did she think she had?

a. 35
b. 29
c. 31
d. 33

13. There were some oranges in a basket, by adding 8/5 of these, the total became 130. How many oranges were in the basket?

a. 60
b. 50
c. 40
d. 35

14. Mr. Brown bought 5 burgers, 3 drinks, 4 fries for his family and a cookie for the dog. If the price of all single items is same, at $1.30 and a 3.5% tax is added, then what is the total cost of dinner?

a. $16.00
b. $16.90
c. $17.00
d. $17.50

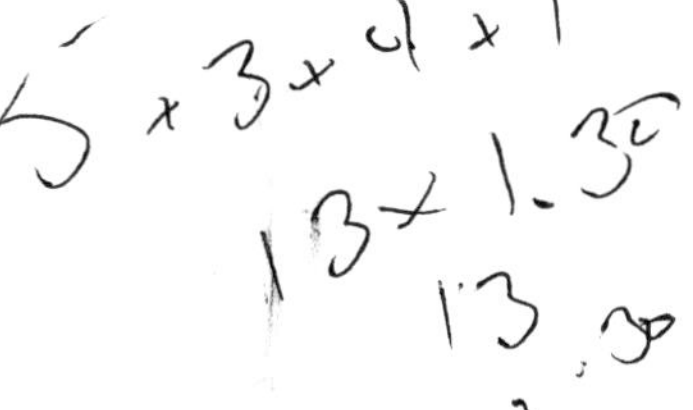

15. A distributor purchased 550 kilograms of potatoes for $165. He distributed these at a rate of $6.4 per 20 kilograms to 15 shops, $3.4 per 10 kilograms to 12 shops and the remainder at $1.8 per 5 kilograms. If his total distribution cost is $10, what will his profit be?

a. $10.40
b. $8.60
c. $14.90
d. $23.40

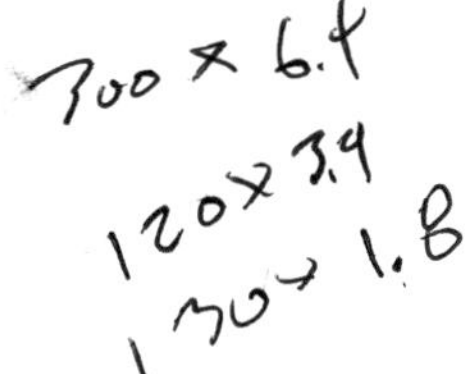

16. Convert 3 yards to feet

a. 18 feet
b. 12 feet
c. 9 feet
d. 27 feet

17. 12t -10 = 14t + 2. Find t

a. -6
b. -4
c. 4
d. 6

18. The price of a book went up from $20 to $25. What percent did the price increase?

a. 5%
b. 10%
c. 20%
d. 25%

19. The price of a book decreased from $25 to $20. What percent did the price decrease?

a. 5%
b. 10%
c. 20%
d. 25%

20. 305 X 25 =

a. 6525
b. 7625
c. 5026
d. 7026

Part IV - Logic

1. Consider the following sequence: 13, 26, 52, 104, ... What number should come next?

a. 208

b. 106

c. 200

d. 400

2. Consider the following sequence: 32, 26, 20, 14, ... What number should come next?

a. 12

b. 19

c. 10

d. 8

3. Consider the following sequence: 12, 4, 16, ..., 36. What is the missing number?

a. 18

b. 22

c. 20

d. 30

Directions: Find the sentence that is true according to the given information.

4. Ben and Ted are classmates. They would ride the school bus together. They also have lunch at the same table. They're even lab partners.

a. Ben and Ted don't like each other.

b. Ben prefers being with other children.

c. Ben and Ted are inseparable.

d. Ted is always alone.

5. Karen takes care of her garden everyday. She grows fruits and vegetables. She always waters them. She also pulls out the weeds and put fertilizer on her plants.

a. Karen hates taking care of her plants.

b. Karen is fond of gardening.

c. Karen plants flowers in her garden.

d. Karen and her mother work on the garden together.

6. Collecting stamps is Tom's hobby. He started collecting stamps when he was six years old. Today, Tom has over a thousand stamps in his collection.

a. Tom collects stamp albums.

b. Tom started collecting stamps in high school.

c. Tom is a stamp collector.

d. Collecting stamps is an expensive hobby.

7. Mother went to market. She bought apples, oranges, and bananas. She also bought cabbage, beans, and squash.

a. Vegetables in the market are expensive.

b. Mother bought chicken and meat.

c. Many people went to the market.

d. Mother bought fruits and vegetables.

8. Tommy and Timmy are brothers. They look the same. They also have the same birthdays.

a. Tommy is older than Timmy.

b. Timmy is more handsome than Tommy.

c. Tommy and Timmy are twins.

d. Tommy and Timmy are best friends.

9. Five students exam marks are posted on a sheet at the front of the class, from lowest at the top, to highest at the bottom.

1. Peter's mark is smaller than Brad's but higher than Emily's mark.
2. Brad's mark is lower that Brittany's.
3. Andrew's mark is third.

Who got the highest mark?

a. Emily

b. Brad

c. Brittany

d. Cannot be determined.

In the code below, the following rules apply:

1. Each letter always represents the same word.
2. Each word is represented by only one letter.
3. The position of a letter and a word in the sentence are never the same.

Z	B	W	O	V	means
Linda	likes	French	lessons	best	

B	C	O	V	E	means
Peter	likes	science	lessons	best	

V	A	G	W	N	means
Linda	does	not	like	algebra	

10. What letter represents Linda?

a. Z
b. B
c. W
d. None of the above.

11. What does 'V' represent?

a. Science
b. Lessons
c. Best
d. Like

Directions: Read the following report and answer questions 12 and 13.

You come on an accident scene on Majestic Ave. A vehicle has been hit and another vehicle, with a damaged front end is fleeing the scene. The vehicle proceeds north on Majestic and turns right on Arbutus St., then left on Oak st., right on Richmond, and then right again on Birch. The vehicle stops on Birch.

12. What direction was the vehicle travelling on Arbutus?

a. North
b. South
c. East
d. West

13. What direction was the vehicle travelling on Richmond?

a. North
b. South
c. East
d. West

14. Arrange the following in the correct sequence.

a. Teens refuse to give their names
b. Several teens flee the scene
c. Dispatch reports a beach party
d. You approach a group of teens

a. CDAB
b. DABC
c. ABCD
d. ADCB

15. Arrange the following in the correct sequence.

a. Robert Smith is charged.
b. A suspect gives his name as Andrew Jones and is released.
c. The suspect is later arrested by other officers.
d. A records check reveals an person fitting his description is actually Robert Smith with a lengthy list of priors.

a. ABCD
b. DCBA
c. CBDA
d. BDCA

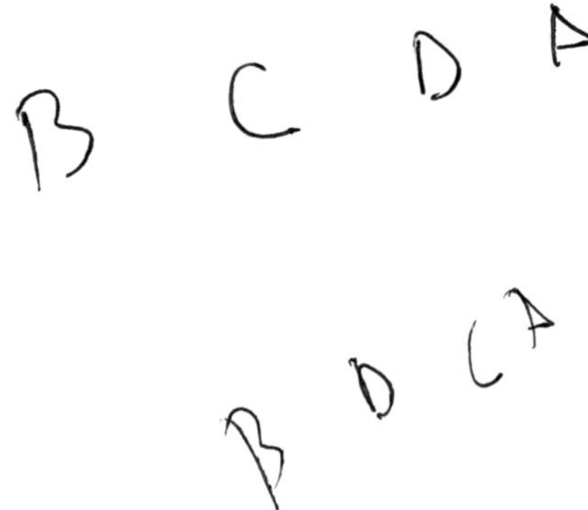

Answer Key

Section III - Reading

1. B
We can infer from this passage that sickness from an infectious disease can be easily transmitted from one person to another.

From the passage, "Infectious pathologies are also called communicable diseases or transmissible diseases, due to their potential of transmission from one person or species to another by a replicating agent (as opposed to a toxin)."

2. A
Two other names for infectious pathologies are communicable diseases and transmissible diseases.

From the passage, "Infectious pathologies are also called communicable diseases or transmissible diseases, due to their potential of transmission from one person or species to another by a replicating agent (as opposed to a toxin)."

3. C
Infectivity describes the ability of an organism to enter, survive and multiply in the host. This is taken directly from the passage, and is a definition type question.

Definition type questions can be answered quickly and easily by scanning the passage for the word you are asked to define.

"Infectivity" is an unusual word, so it is quick and easy to scan the passage looking for this word.

4. B
We know an infection is not synonymous with an infectious disease because an infection may not cause important clinical symptoms or impair host function.

5. C
We can infer from the passage that, a virus is too small to be seen with the naked eye. Clearly, if they are too small to be seen with a microscope, then they are too small to be seen with the naked eye.

6. D
Viruses infect all types of organisms. This is taken directly from the passage, "Viruses infect all types of organisms, from animals and plants to bacteria and single-celled organisms."

7. C
The passage does not say exactly how many parts prions and viroids consist of. It does say, "**Unlike** prions and viroids, viruses consist of two or three parts ..." so prions and viroids are NOT like virus. We can therefore infer, they consist of either less than two or more than three parts.

8. B
A common virus spread by coughing and sneezing is influenza.

9. C
The cumulus stage of a thunderstorm is the beginning of the thunderstorm.

This is taken directly from the passage, "The first stage of a thunderstorm is the cumulus, or developing stage."

10. D
The passage lists four ways that air is heated. One way is, heat created by water vapor condensing into liquid.

11. A
The sequence of events can be taken from these sentences:

As the moisture carried by the [1] air currents rises, it rapidly cools into liquid drops of water, which appear as cumulus clouds. As the water vapor condenses into liquid, it [2] releases heat, which warms the air. This in turn causes the air to become less dense than the surrounding dry air and [3] rise farther.

12. C

The purpose of this text is to explain when meteorologists consider a thunderstorm severe.

The main idea is the first sentence, "The United States National Weather Service classifies thunderstorms as severe when they reach a predetermined level." After the first sentence, the passage explains and elaborates on this idea. Everything is this passage is related to this idea, and there are no other major ideas in this passage that are central to the whole passage.

13. A

From this passage, we can infer that different areas and countries have different criteria for determining a severe storm.

From the passage we can see that most of the US has a criteria of, winds over 50 knots (58 mph or 93 km/h), and hail ¾ inch (2 cm). For the Central US, hail must be 1 inch (2.5 cm) in diameter. In Canada, winds must be 90 km/h or greater, hail 2 centimeters in diameter or greater, and rainfall more than 50 millimeters in 1 hour, or 75 millimeters in 3 hours.

Choice D is incorrect because the Canadian system is the same for hail, 2 centimeters in diameter.

14. C

With hail above the minimum size of 2.5 cm. diameter, the Central Region of the United States National Weather Service would issue a severe thunderstorm warning.

15. A

A tornado warning is issued where this is a funnel cloud or tornado, even though there may be a severe thunderstorm.

16. C

This question tests the reader's vocabulary skills. The uses of the negatives "but" and "less," especially right next to each other, may confuse readers into answering with choices A or D, which list words that are antonyms to "militant." Readers may also be confused by the comparison of healthy people with what is being described as an overly healthy person-

-both people are good, but the reader may look for which one is "worse" in the comparison, and therefore stray toward the antonym words. One key to understanding the meaning of "militant" if the reader is unfamiliar with it is to look at the root of the word; readers can then easily associate it with "military" and gain a sense of what the word signifies: defense (especially considered that the immune system defends the body). Choice C is correct over choice B because "militant" is an adjective, just as the words in choice C, whereas the words in choices B are nouns.

17. C

This question tests the reader's understanding of function within writing. The other choices are details included surrounding the quoted text, and may therefore confuse the reader. Choice A somewhat contradicts what is said earlier in the paragraph, which is, tests and treatments are improving, and probably doctors are along with them, but the paragraph doesn't actually mention doctors, and the subject of the question is the medicine. Choice B may seem correct to readers who aren't careful to understand that, while the author does mention the large number of people affected, the author is touching on the realities of living with allergies, rather than about the likelihood of curing all allergies. Similarly, while the author does mention the "balance" of the body, which is easily associated with "wholesome," the author is not really making an argument and especially is not making an extreme statement that allergy medicines should be outlawed. Again, because the article's tone is on living with allergies, choice C is an appropriate choice that fits with the title and content of the text.

18. B

This question tests the reader's inference skills. The text does not state who is doing the recommending, but the use of the "patients," as well as the general context of the passage, lends itself to the logical partner, "doctors," in choice B. The author does mention the recommendation but doesn't present it as her own (i.e. "I recommend that"), so choice A may be eliminated. It may seem plausible that people with allergies (D) may recommend medicines or products to other people with allergies, but the text does not necessarily support this interaction taking place. Choice C may be selected because the

EpiPen is specifically mentioned, but the use of the phrase "such as" when it is introduced is not limiting enough to assume the recommendation is coming from its creators.

19. D
This question tests the reader's global understanding of the text. Choice D includes the main topics of the three body paragraphs, and isn't too focused on a specific aspect or quote from the text, as the other questions are, giving a skewed summary of what the author intended. The reader may be drawn to choice B because of the title of the passage and the use of words like "better," but the message of the passage is larger and more general than this.

20. C
The main idea is the first sentence of the passage; a cloud is a visible mass of droplets or frozen crystals floating in the atmosphere above the surface of the Earth or other planetary body.

The main idea is very often the first sentence of the paragraph.

Part II - Observation, Professional Judgement, Recognition and Identification.

Professional Judgement

1. D
The priority is safety, so checking the wife is the first thing, then subdue the man.

2. B
There is no reason to release the man as he has caused significant damage.

3. D
The first priority is the ensure safety, then to interview both men separately.

4. B
If the suspect is willing to provide information about another crime, then take the information, but this cannot be bartered for release after arrest.

5. B
Under no circumstances should the suspect drive his own car.

6. A
The safest course of action is the wait for backup.

7. B
The safest action is the approach the beach party and ask if they know anything about the vandalized cars, and your next response will depend on their reaction and information.

8. D
Give your name and badge number and give him a ticket.

9. B
The first objective is to assess the woman's injuries and call for an ambulance if necessary.

10. B
The first responsibility is to the unconscious owner. After, or while assessing the unconscious owner, call update dispatch of the whole situation.

Recognition and Identification

11. A
Choice A has the same face but different hair. The other suspects have much thinner, or different shaped faces.

12. C
Choice C is the same person wearing sunglasses. The suspect's face in choices A and D are much thinner and the suspect in choice B is wider.

13. C
The suspects in choices A and B have a thinner face, and the suspect in choice D has a wider face.

Observation

14. D
William Jackson does not have any identifying marks.

15. B
Kenneth Walker is wanted for armed robbery.

16. A
The Porche Carrera is wanted for dangerous driving.

17. B
The Smart Car is from New Brunswick.

18. A
Steven Hermandez is wanted for theft of a motor vehicle.

19. C
Linda Moore has tatoos on her left forearm.

20. B
The Volkwagen Beetle is yellow.

Composition

1. C
Dauntless: adj. Invulnerable to fear or intimidation.

2. A
Juxtaposed: adj. Placed side by side often for comparison or contrast.

3. B
Regicide: v. killing of a king.

4. A
Pernicious: adj. Causing much harm in a subtle way.

5. A
Immune: adj. Resistant to a particular infection or toxin owing to the presence of specific antibodies.

6. B
Nimble: adj. Quick and light in movement or action. Agile.

7. A
Queries: n. Questions or inquiries.

8. C
Depose: To remove (a leader) from (high) office, without killing the incumbent.

9. D
Pedestrian: Ordinary, dull; everyday; unexceptional.

10. B
Petulant: adj. Childishly irritable.

11. C
Humorous is the correct spelling.

12. B
Knowledge is the correct spelling.

13. A
Camaraderie is the correct spelling.

14. A
Mathematics is the correct spelling.

15. C
Conscientious is the correct spelling.

16. D
Leisure is the correct spelling.

17. C
Pigeon is the correct spelling.

18. D
Odyssey is the correct spelling.

19. C
Sacrilegious is the correct spelling.

20. A
Accommodate is the correct spelling.

21. C
The major words in the titles of books, articles, and songs are capitalized. (but not short prepositions or the articles "the," "a," or "an," if they are not the first word of the title)

22. A
Titles of publications are capitalized.

23. A
Singular subjects. "The Chinese" is plural, and "a citizen of Bermuda" is singular.

24. A
Disease is singular.

25. C
Articles of speech. Both dog and cat in this sentence are singular and require the article 'a.'

26. B
Former vs. Latter. 'Former' refers to the first of two things, 'latter' to the second.

27. B
Fewer vs. Less. 'Fewer' is used with countables and 'less' is used with un-countables.

28. A
'However' usage. 'However' usually has a comma before and after.

29. D
'However' Usage. 'However' usually has a comma before and after.

30. A
The third conditional is used for talking about an unreal

situation (that did not happen) in the past. For example, "If I had studied harder, [if clause] I would have passed the exam [main clause]. Which is the same as, "I failed the exam, because I didn't study hard enough."

Part IV – Mathematics

1. A
1/3 X 3/4 = 3/12 = 1/4

2. D
75/1500 = 15/300 = 3/60 = 1/20

3. D
3.14 + 2.73 = 5.87 and 5.87 + 23.7 = 29.57

4. B
Spent 15% - 100% - 15% = 85%

5. C
125 : 500 is the same as 25 : 100 or 1 : 4. So the amount of salt will be 0.75/4 = 0.1875, or about .19 grams.

6. B
Total expenses = 5284.34 + $8,384.76 + $2,920.00 = $16,589.10

Profit = revenue less expenses

$19,304.56 - 16589.10 = $2,715.46

7. A
$5,000 at 4% = 5000 X 4/100
5000 X .4 = 200
So the total after one year will be $5,200

8. C
If each bus carries 36 students, and there are 144 students total, then 144/36 = 4 buses.

9. D
If a square is 5 feet tall, then the area will be 5 X 5 = 25.

10. D
Since there are 12 months in a year = 12 possibilities, the chance of guessing the correct month will be 1 in 12.

11. B
John's total will be 40% of 8.50 plus the tip of $1.30.

8.5 X 4/100 = 8.5 X .4 = 3.40

Total = 3.40 + 1.30 = $4.70.

12. D
If she has $8.75, that will equal 35 quarters. ($8.00 = 32 quarters and $.75 = 3 quarters, total 35 quarters).

She had 2 more quarters than she thought, so she had 35 - 2 = 33 quarters.

13. B
Suppose oranges in the basket before = x, Then: X + 8x/5 = 130, 5x + 8x = 650, so X = 50.

14. D
As price of all the single items is same and there are 13 total items. So the total cost will be 13 × 1.3 = $16.90. After 3.5 percent tax this amount will become 16.9×1.035=$17.50.

15. B
The distribution is done in three different rates and amounts:

$6.4 per 20 kilograms to 15 shops ... 20•15 = 300 kilograms distributed

$3.4 per 10 kilograms to 12 shops ... 10•12 = 120 kilograms distributed

550 - (300 + 120) = 550 - 420 = 130 kilograms left. This amount is distributed by 5 kilogram portions. So, this means that there are 130/5 = 26 shops.

$1.8 per 130 kilograms.

We need to find the amount he earned overall these distributions.

$6.4 per 20 kilograms : 6.4•15 = $96 for 300 kilograms

$3.4 per 10 kilograms : 3.4•12 = $40.8 for 120 kilograms

$1.8 per 5 kilograms : 1.8•26 = $46.8 for 130 kilograms

So, he earned 96 + 40.8 + 46.8 = $ 183.6

The total distribution cost is given as $10

The profit is found by: Money earned - money spent ... It is important to remember that he bought 550 kilograms of potatoes for $165 at the beginning:

Profit = 183.6 - 10 - 165 = $8.6

16. C
1 yard = 3 feet, 3 yards = 3 feet x 3 = 9 feet

17. C
12t -10 = 14t + 2

Collect terms with the same variable on the same side, switching to negative if you bring terms over the equals sign.

-2t - 10 = 2

Collect number on the same side switching to negative if you bring terms over the equals sign.

-2t = -8

Divide both sides by -2.
-t = -4
t = 4

18. D
Price increased by $5 ($25-$20). The percent increase is 5/20 x 100 = 5 x 5 = 25%

19. C
Price decreased by $5 ($25-$20). The percent increase = 5/25 x 100 = 5 x 4 = 20%

20. B
305 X 25 = 7625

Part V - Logic

1. A
The number doubles each time.

2. D
The numbers decrease by 6 each time.

3. C
Each number is the sum of the previous two numbers.

4. C
The only certain thing is Ben and Ted are inseparable.

5. B
The only certain thing is Karen is fond of gardening.

6. C
The only certain thing is Tom is a stamp collector.

7. D
The only certain thing is mother bought fruits and vegetables.

8. C
The only certain thing is they are twins.

9. C
Brittany's mark is the highest.

According to condition 1, the order is:

Emily
Peter
Brad

With condition 2,

Emily
Peter
Brad
Brittany

With condition 3,

Emily
Peter
Andrew
Brad
Brittany

The list is from lowest at the top to highest at the bottom, so Brittany's mark is the highest.

10. C
Linda appears in the first and third sentence and so do 'Z' and 'W,' so it must be one of the two. 'Z' is in the same position as Linda in the first sentence and can be eliminated, so Linda must be 'W.'

11. D
'Like' is in all three sentences, so it must be 'B,' 'O' or 'V.' The only one of these three to appear in the third sentence is 'V,' so it must be 'like.'

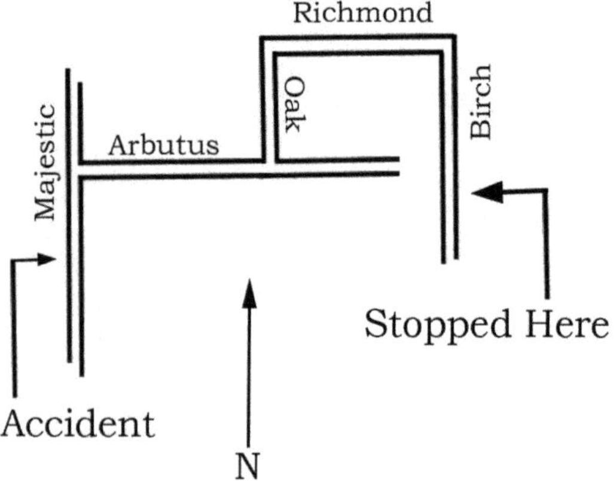

12. C
The vehicle was travelling east on Arbutus.

13. C
The vehicle was travelling east on Richmond.

14. A
C, D, A, B is the correct sequence.

c. Dispatch reports a beach party

d. You approach a group of teens

a. Teens refuse to give their names

b. Several teens flee the scene

15. D
B, D, C, A is the correct sequence.

b. A suspect gives his name as Andrew Jones and is released.

d. A records check reveals an person fitting his description is actually Robert Smith with a lengthy list of priors.

c. The suspect is later arrested by other officers.
a. Robert Smith is charged.

Practice Test Questions Set 2

The questions below are not the same as you will find on the RCMP - that would be too easy! And nobody knows what the questions will be and they change all the time. Below are general questions that cover the same subject areas as the RCMP. So the format and exact wording of the questions may differ slightly, and change from year to year, if you can answer the questions below, you will have no problem with the RCMP.

For the best results, take these Practice Test Questions as if it were the real exam. Set aside time when you will not be disturbed, and a location that is quiet and free of distractions. Read the instructions carefully, read each question carefully, and answer to the best of your ability.
Use the bubble answer sheets provided. When you have completed the Practice Questions, check your answer against the Answer Key and read the explanation provided.

Do not attempt more than one set of practice test questions in one day. After completing the first practice test, wait two or three days before attempting the second set of questions.

Reading Comprehension - 20 Questions

Observation – 7 Questions

Professional Judgement: 10 Questions

Recognition/Identification – 3 Questions

Composition – 20 questions

Math - 20 questions

Logic – 20 questions

Reading Comprehension

1.	A	B	C	D	11.	A	B	C	D
2.	A	B	C	D	12.	A	B	C	D
3.	A	B	C	D	13.	A	B	C	D
4.	A	B	C	D	14.	A	B	C	D
5.	A	B	C	D	15.	A	B	C	D
6.	A	B	C	D	16.	A	B	C	D
7.	A	B	C	D	17.	A	B	C	D
8.	A	B	C	D	18.	A	B	C	D
9.	A	B	C	D	19.	A	B	C	D
10.	A	B	C	D	20.	A	B	C	D

Observation, Professional Judgment, Recognition and Identification

1. (A) (B) (C) (D)
2. (A) (B) (C) (D)
3. (A) (B) (C) (D)
4. (A) (B) (C) (D)
5. (A) (B) (C) (D)
6. (A) (B) (C) (D)
7. (A) (B) (C) (D)
8. (A) (B) (C) (D)
9. (A) (B) (C) (D)
10. (A) (B) (C) (D)
11. (A) (B) (C) (D)
12. (A) (B) (C) (D)
13. (A) (B) (C) (D)
14. (A) (B) (C) (D)
15. (A) (B) (C) (D)
16. (A) (B) (C) (D)
17. (A) (B) (C) (D)
18. (A) (B) (C) (D)
19. (A) (B) (C) (D)
20. (A) (B) (C) (D)

Composition

1. (A) (B) (C) (D)
2. (A) (B) (C) (D)
3. (A) (B) (C) (D)
4. (A) (B) (C) (D)
5. (A) (B) (C) (D)
6. (A) (B) (C) (D)
7. (A) (B) (C) (D)
8. (A) (B) (C) (D)
9. (A) (B) (C) (D)
10. (A) (B) (C) (D)
11. (A) (B) (C) (D)
12. (A) (B) (C) (D)
13. (A) (B) (C) (D)
14. (A) (B) (C) (D)
15. (A) (B) (C) (D)
16. (A) (B) (C) (D)
17. (A) (B) (C) (D)
18. (A) (B) (C) (D)
19. (A) (B) (C) (D)
20. (A) (B) (C) (D)

Math

1. (A) (B) (C) (D)
2. (A) (B) (C) (D)
3. (A) (B) (C) (D)
4. (A) (B) (C) (D)
5. (A) (B) (C) (D)
6. (A) (B) (C) (D)
7. (A) (B) (C) (D)
8. (A) (B) (C) (D)
9. (A) (B) (C) (D)
10. (A) (B) (C) (D)
11. (A) (B) (C) (D)
12. (A) (B) (C) (D)
13. (A) (B) (C) (D)
14. (A) (B) (C) (D)
15. (A) (B) (C) (D)
16. (A) (B) (C) (D)
17. (A) (B) (C) (D)
18. (A) (B) (C) (D)
19. (A) (B) (C) (D)
20. (A) (B) (C) (D)

Logic

1.	A	B	C	D	11.	A	B	C	D
2.	A	B	C	D	12.	A	B	C	D
3.	A	B	C	D	13.	A	B	C	D
4.	A	B	C	D	14.	A	B	C	D
5.	A	B	C	D	15.	A	B	C	D
6.	A	B	C	D	16.	A	B	C	D
7.	A	B	C	D	17.	A	B	C	D
8.	A	B	C	D	18.	A	B	C	D
9.	A	B	C	D	19.	A	B	C	D
10.	A	B	C	D	20.	A	B	C	D

Part I - Reading Comprehension

Questions 1 - 4 refer to the following passage.

Passage 1 - The Respiratory System

The respiratory system's function is to allow oxygen exchange through all parts of the body. The anatomy or structure of the exchange system, and the uses of the exchanged gases, varies depending on the organism. In humans and other mammals, for example, the anatomical features of the respiratory system include airways, lungs, and the respiratory muscles. Molecules of oxygen and carbon dioxide are passively exchanged, by diffusion, between the gaseous external environment and the blood. This exchange occurs in the alveolar region of the lungs.

Other animals, such as insects, have respiratory systems with very simple anatomical features, and in amphibians even the skin plays a vital role in gas exchange. Plants also have respiratory systems but the direction of gas exchange can be opposite to that of animals.

The respiratory system can also be divided into physiological, or functional, zones. These include the conducting zone (the region for gas transport from the outside atmosphere to just above the alveoli), the transitional zone, and the respiratory zone (the alveolar region where gas exchange occurs). [9]

1. What can we infer from the first paragraph in this passage?

a. Human and mammal respiratory systems are the same.

b. The lungs are an important part of the respiratory system.

c. The respiratory system varies in different mammals.

d. Oxygen and carbon dioxide are passive exchanged by the respiratory system.

2. What is the process by which molecules of oxygen and carbon dioxide are passively exchanged?

a. Transfusion
b. Affusion
c. Diffusion
d. Respiratory confusion

3. What organ plays an important role in gas exchange in amphibians?

a. The skin
b. The lungs
c. The gills
d. The mouth

4. What are the three physiological zones of the respiratory system?

a. Conducting, transitional, respiratory zones
b. Redacting, transitional, circulatory zones
c. Conducting, circulatory, inhibiting zones
d. Transitional, inhibiting, conducting zones

Questions 5 – 7 refer to the following passage.

Passage 2 – Mythology

The main characters in myths are usually gods or supernatural heroes. As sacred stories, rulers and priests have traditionally endorsed their myths and as a result, myths have a close link with religion and politics. In the society where a myth originates, the natives believe the myth is a true account of the remote past. In fact, many societies have two categories of traditional narrative—(1) "true stories," or myths, and (2) "false stories," or fables.

Myths generally take place during a primordial age, when the world was still young, before achieving its current form. These stories explain how the world gained its current form and why the culture developed its customs, institutions, and taboos. Closely related to myth are legend and folktale. Myths, legends, and folktales are different types of traditional stories. Unlike myths, folktales can take place at any time and any place, and the natives do not usually consider them true or sacred. Legends, on the other hand, are similar to myths in that many people have traditionally considered them true. Legends take place in a more recent time, when the world was much as it is today. In addition, legends generally feature humans as their main characters, whereas myths have superhuman characters. [10]

5. We can infer from this passage that

a. Folktales took place in a time far past, before civilization covered the earth.

b. Humankind uses myth to explain how the world was created.

c. Myths revolve around gods or supernatural beings; the local community usually accepts these stories as not true.

d. The only difference between a myth and a legend is the time setting of the story.

6. The main purpose of this passage is

a. To distinguish between many types of traditional stories, and explain the back-ground of some traditional story categories.

b. To determine whether myths and legends might be true accounts of history.

c. To show the importance of folktales how these traditional stories made life more bearable in harder times.

d. None of the Above.

7. How are folktales different from myths?

a. Folktales and myth are the same.

b. Folktales are not true and generally not sacred and take place anytime.

c. Myths are not true and generally not sacred and take place anytime.

d. Folktales explained the formation of the world and myths do not.

Questions 8 - 11 refer to the following passage.

Passage 3 – Myths, Legend and Folklore

Cultural historians draw a distinction between myth, legend and folktale simply as a way to group traditional stories. However, in many cultures, drawing a sharp line between myths and legends is not that simple. Instead of dividing their traditional stories into myths, legends, and folktales, some cultures divide them into two categories. The first category roughly corresponds to folktales, and the second is one that combines myths and legends. Similarly, we cannot always separate myths from folktales. One society might consider a story true, making it a myth. Another society may believe the story is fiction, which makes it a folktale. In fact, when a myth loses its status as part of a religious system, it often takes on traits more typical of folktales, with its formerly divine characters now appearing as human heroes, giants, or fairies. Myth, legend, and folktale are only a few of the categories of traditional stories. Other categories include anecdotes and some kinds of jokes. Traditional stories, in turn, are only one category within the larger category of folklore, which also includes items such as gestures, costumes, and music. [10]

8. The main idea of this passage is that

a. Myths, fables, and folktales are not the same thing, and each describes a specific type of story.

b. Traditional stories can be categorized in different ways by different people.

c. Cultures use myths for religious purposes, and when this is no longer true, the people forget and discard these myths.

d. Myths can never become folk tales, because one is true, and the other is false.

9. The terms myth and legend are

a. Categories that are synonymous with true and false.

b. Categories that group traditional stories according to certain characteristics.

c. Interchangeable, because both terms mean a story that is passed down from generation to generation.

d. Meant to distinguish between a story that involves a hero and a cultural message and a story meant only to entertain.

10. Traditional story categories not only include myths and legends, but

a. Can also include gestures, since some cultures passed these down before the written and spoken word.

b. In addition, folklore refers to stories involving fables and fairy tales.

c. These story categories can also include folk music and traditional dress.

d. Traditional stories themselves are a part of the larger category of folklore, which may also include costumes, gestures, and music.

11. This passage shows that

a. There is a distinct difference between a myth and a legend, although both are folktales.

b. Myths are folktales, but folktales are not myths.

c. Myths, legends, and folktales play an important part in tradition and the past, and are a rich and colorful part of history.

d. Most cultures consider myths to be true.

Questions 12 - 15 refer to the following passage.

Passage 4 – Ways Characters Communicate in Theater

Playwrights give their characters voices in a way that gives depth and added meaning to what happens on stage during their play. There are different types of speech in scripts that allow characters to talk with themselves, with other characters, and even with the audience.

It is very unique to theater that characters may talk "to themselves." When characters do this, the speech they give is called a soliloquy. Soliloquies are usually poetic, introspective, moving, and can tell audience members about the feelings, motivations, or suspicions of an individual character without that character having to reveal them to other characters on stage. "To be or not to be" is a famous soliloquy given by Hamlet as he considers difficult but important themes, such as life and death.

The most common type of communication in plays is when one character is speaking to another or a group of other characters. This is generally called dialogue, but can also be called monologue if one character speaks without being interrupted for a long time. It is not necessarily the most important type of communication, but it is the most common because the plot of the play cannot really progress without it.

Lastly, and most unique to theater (although it has been

used somewhat in film) is when a character speaks directly to the audience. This is called an aside, and scripts usually specifically direct actors to do this. Asides are usually comical, an inside joke between the character and the audience, and very short. The actor will usually face the audience when delivering them, even if it's for a moment, so the audience can recognize this move as an aside.

All three of these types of communication are important to the art of theater, and have been perfected by famous playwrights like Shakespeare. Understanding these types of communication can help an audience member grasp what is artful about the script and action of a play.

12. According to the passage, characters in plays communicate to

a. move the plot forward.

b. show the private thoughts and feelings of one character.

c. make the audience laugh.

d. add beauty and artistry to the play.

13. When Hamlet delivers "To be or not to be," he can most likely be described as

a. solitary

b. thoughtful

c. dramatic

d. hopeless

14. The author uses parentheses to punctuate "although it has been used somewhat in film"

a. to show that films are less important

b. instead of using commas so that the sentence is not interrupted

c. because parenthesis help separate details that are not as important

d. to show that films are not as artistic

15. It can be understood that by the phrase "give their characters voices," the author means that

a. playwrights are generous.

b. playwrights are changing the sound or meaning of characters' voices to fit what they had in mind.

c. dialogue is important in creating characters.

d. playwrights may be the parent of one of their actors and literally give them their voice.

Questions 16 - 17 refer to the following passage.

Passage 5 – Trees II

With an estimated 100,000 species, trees represent 25 percent of all living plant species. Most tree species grow in tropical regions of the world and many of these areas have not been surveyed by botanists, making species diversity poorly understood. The earliest trees were tree ferns and horsetails, which grew in forests in the Carboniferous period. Tree ferns still survive, but the only surviving horsetails are no longer in tree form. Later, in the Triassic period, conifers and ginkgos, appeared, followed by flowering plants after that in the Cretaceous period. [11]

16. What tree(s) survived from the Carboniferous period?

a. 25% of all trees
b. Horsetails
c. Conifers
d. Tree Ferns

17. Choose the correct list below, ranked from oldest to youngest trees.

a. Flowering plants, conifers and ginkgos, tree ferns and horsetails.
b. Tree ferns and horsetails, conifers and ginkgos, flowering plants.
c. Tree ferns and horsetails, flowering plants, conifers and ginkgos.
d. Conifers and ginkgos, tree ferns and horsetails, flowering plants.

Questions 18 - 20 refer to the following passage.

Passage 6 - Women and Advertising

Only in the last few generations have media messages been so widespread and so readily seen, heard, and read by so many people. Advertising is an important part of both selling and buying anything from soap to cereal to jeans. For whatever reason, more consumers are women than are men. Media message are subtle but powerful, and more attention has been paid lately to how these message affect women.

Of all the products that women buy, makeup, clothes, and other stylistic or cosmetic products are among the most popular. This means that companies focus their advertising on women, promising them that their product will make her feel, look, or smell better than the next company's product will. This competition has resulted in advertising that is more and more ideal and less and less possible for everyday women. However, because women do look to these ideals and the products they represent as how they can potentially become, many women have developed unhealthy attitudes about themselves when they have failed to become those ideals.

In recent years, more companies have tried to change advertisements to be healthier for women. This includes featuring models of more sizes and addressing a huge outcry against unfair tools such as airbrushing and photo editing. There is considerable debate over the right balance between real and ideal is, because fashion is also considered art and some changes are made to elevate purposefully fashionable products and signify that they are creative, innovative, and the work of individual people. Artists want their freedom protected as much as women do, and advertising agencies are often caught in the middle.

Some claim that the companies who make these changes are not doing enough. Many people worry that there are still not enough models of different sizes and different ethnicities. Some people claim that companies use this healthier type of advertisement not for the good of women, but because they would like to sell products to the women who are looking for these kinds of messages. This is also a hard balance to find: companies do need to make money, and women do need to feel respected.

While the focus of this change has been on women, advertising can also affect men, and this change will hopefully be a lesson on media for all consumers.

18. The second paragraph states that advertising focuses on women

a. to shape what the ideal should be.
b. because women buy makeup.
c. because women are easily persuaded.
d. because of the types of products that women buy.

19. According to the passage, fashion artists and female consumers are at odds because

a. there is a debate going on and disagreement drives people apart.

b. both of them are trying to protect their freedom to do something.

c. artists want to elevate their products above the reach of women.

d. women are creative, innovative, individual people.

20. The author uses the phrase "for whatever reason" in this passage to

a. keep the focus of the paragraph on media messages and not on the differences between men and women.

b. show that the reason for this is unimportant.

c. argue that it is stupid that more women are consumers than men.

d. show that he or she is tired of talking about why media messages are important.

Part II - Observation, Professional Judgement, Recognition and Identification

Directions: You have five minutes to memorize the following information. Do not write anything down. Questions follow on page 228.

Name: Janet Benoit
Description: Caucasian female with shoulder length hair. Heart tattoo on right arm.

Wanted for: Child neglect

Name: Robby Valence

Description: 5 ft 5 in Caucasian male, stocky build, no identifying marks

Wanted for: Armed Robbery

Make and Model: Volkswagen Passat

Licence: British Columbia MN1 23C

Wanted in Connection with: Dangerous Driving

Make and Model: Volkswagen Phaeton

Licence: Ontario MUYR-123

Wanted in Connection with: Fraud

Name: Nathan Abraham

Description: Black Canadian Male, 5 ft 1 in. no identifying features

Wanted for: Domestic Assault

Name: Jeffrey Crisp

Description: 5 ft 6 in Caucasian male, slight build, no identifying marks

Wanted for: Sexual Assault

Make and Model: Modified Honda Accord

Licence: Quebec A12 BRP

Wanted for: Homicide

Make and Model: Modified Chevrolet Truck

Licence: Yukon RTJ12

Wanted in Connection with: Uttering Threats

Professional Judgment

Scenario: You are called to a robbery and see two cars leaving the scene at high speed. You give chase, however, the cars are driving at very high speed and driving very dangerously.

1. What should you do?

a. Call dispatch with as much information as possible

b. Follow the cars and match their speed.

c. Follow the cars at a high but safe speed, even if you fall behind

d. Follow the cars but do not exceed the speed limit.

Scenario: You are in a meeting with several colleagues from a neighboring municipality, discussing the events of last night. A radio call comes in reporting an officer needing assistance. The location is very close to your station.

2. What should you do?

a. Continue with the meeting as others officers will respond.

b. Leave the meeting immediately and respond to the call

c. Invite the other officers to respond to the call with you

d. Wrap up the meeting early and respond to the call

Scenario: You attend a noise complaint and are questioning several teenagers. They have numerous chocolate bars in their pockets and there are chocolate bar wrappers on the ground around them. The teenagers refuse to speak with you unless you arrest them.

3. What should you do?

a. Call the station and ask if there has been any thefts nearby

b. Arrest the teenagers

c. Demand that they provide you with their names

d. Accuse them of stealing the chocolate bars

Scenario: You are on your lunch break in a local restaurant with your partner. A person approaches you in a panic saying there is a man having a heart attack in the next building.

4. What should you do?

a. Politely tell the person you are having lunch but will radio in the call.

b. Leave lunch immediately and investigate the report

c. Finish you lunch and tell your junior partner to attend to the complaint

d. Ignore the complaint

Scenario: You apprehend a black suspect apparently leaving the scene of a break and enter. The suspect accuses you of racial profiling.

5. What should you do?

a. Release the suspect to avoid an ugly scene

b. Deny the accusation and continue

c. Explain that you have found him apparently leaving the scene of a crime and would like to ask some questions

d. Explain the police policy on racial profiling

The black suspect still insists that you are stopping his because of his race and refuses to answer any questions.

What should you do?

a. You have already explained that you have found him at the scene of a break and enter, and would like to ask some questions. The next step is to explain that if he continues to refuse, you will have to take him to the station for questioning.

b. Arrest him immediately

c. Explain the situation again

d. Avoid an ugly scene and allow him to go

Scenario: You are patrolling a local street and find a couple having a heated argument.

7. What should you do?

a. Tell the couple to stop arguing

b. Ask if everything is OK

c. Listen to the argument and try to resolve

d. Listen to the argument and take the side of the best argument

Recognition and Identification

8. Choose the person that matches the suspect below.

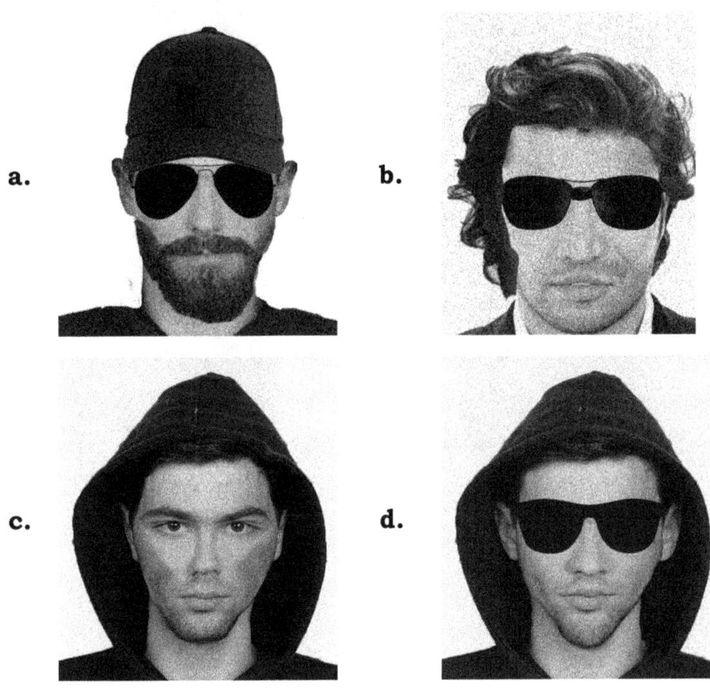

9. Choose the person that matches the suspect below.

a. 

b. 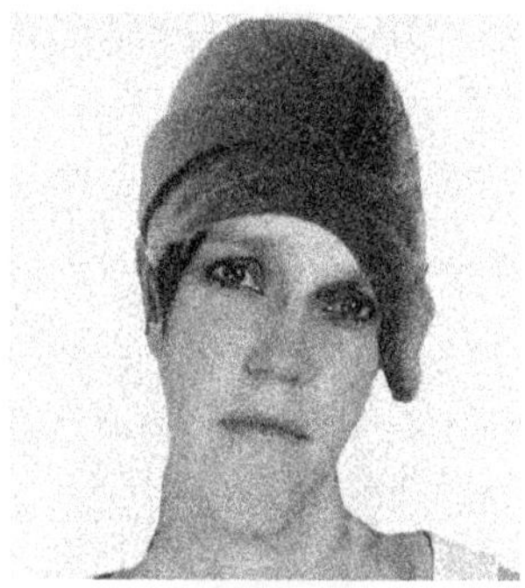

c. 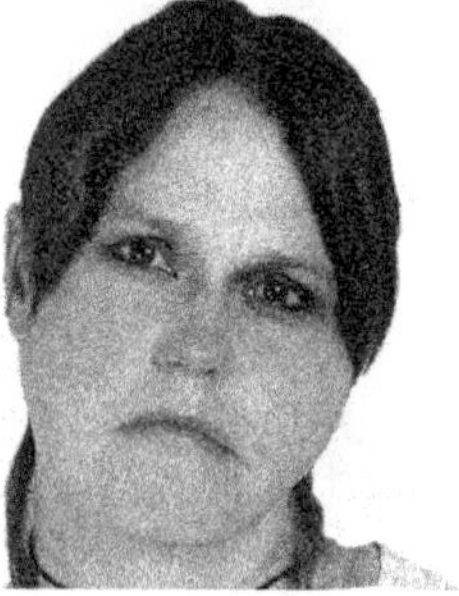

d. 

10. Choose the person that matches the suspect below.

a.

b.

c.

d.

Observation

Questions 11 - 15 refer to the information on pages 216 - 219.

11. Who is wanted for child neglect?

a. Robby Valence
b. Janet Benoit
c. Jeffrey Crisp
d. Nathan Abraham

12. Who is wanted for sexual assault?

a. Robby Valence
b. Janet Benoit
c. Jeffrey Crisp
d. Nathan Abraham

13. What province is the Volkswagen Phaeton from?

a. Yukon
b. Quebec
c. Ontario
c. British Columbia

14. What is Nathan Abraham wanted for?

a. Sexual Assault
b. Armed Robbery
c. Child Neglect
d. Domestic Assault

15. What province is the modified Chevrolet truck from?

a. Yukon
b. Quebec
c. Ontario
c. British Columbia

Part III - Composition

1. Choose the best definition of anecdote.

a. A short account of an incident
b. Something that comes before
c. The use of humour, irony, exaggeration, or ridicule
d. Constant fluctuations

2. Choose the adjective that means shocking, terrible or wicked.

a. Pleasantries
b. Heinous
c. Shrewd
d. Provencal

3. Choose the noun that means a person or thing that tells or announces the coming of someone or something.

a. Harbinger
b. Evasion
c. Bleak
d. Craven

4. Choose a word that means the same as the underlined word.

He wasn't especially generous. All the servings were very judicious.

a. Abundant

b. Careful

c. Extravagant

d. Careless

5. Fill in the blank.

Because of the growing use of ________as a fuel, corn production has greatly increased.

a. Alcohol

b. Ethanol

c. Natural gas

d. Oil

6. Fill in the blank.

In heavily industrialized areas, the pollution of the air causes many to develop ________ diseases.

a. Respiratory

b. Cardiac

c. Alimentary

d. Circulatory

7. Choose the best definition of inherent.

a. To receive money in a will

b. An essential part of

c. To receive money from a will

d. None of the above

8. Choose the best definition of vapid.

a. adj. tasteless or bland
b. v. To inflict, as a revenge or punishment
c. v. to convert into gas
d. v. to go up in smoke

9. Choose the best definition of waif.

a. n. a sick and hungry child
b. n. an orphan staying in a foster home
c. n. homeless child or stray
d. n. a type of French bread eaten with cheese

10. Choose the adjective that means similar or identical.

a. Soluble
b. Assembly
c. Conclave
d. Homologous

11. Choose the correct spelling.

a. Correspondence
b. Corespodence
c. Correspodence
d. Correspomdence

12. Choose the correct spelling.

a. Henmorrhage
b. Hemmorrhage
c. Hemorrhage
d. Hemorhage

13. Choose the correct spelling.

a. Envirommnment
b. Environment
c. Environiment
d. Enviromment

14. Choose the correct spelling.

a. Govermment
b. Goverment
c. Govenment
d. Government

15. Choose the correct spelling.

a. Conceeve
b. Concieve
c. Conceive
d. Conceve

16. Choose the correct spelling.

a. Describe
b. Decribe
c. Decsribe
d. Discribe

17. Choose the correct spelling.

a. Liqour
b. Liquor
c. Liquer
d. Liquour

18. Choose the correct spelling.

a. Succesful
b. Sucessful
c. Sucessfull
d. Successful

19. Choose the correct spelling.

a. Huricane
b. Hurricane
c. Huricane
d. Hurriccane

20. Choose the correct spelling.

a. Precede
b. Preccede
c. Precceed
d. Preceed

21. Choose the sentence below with the correct punctuation.

a. There are many species of owls, the Great-Horned Owl, the Snowy Owl, and the Western Screech Owl, and the Barn Owl.

b. There are many species of owls, the Great-Horned Owl: the Snowy Owl: and the Western Screech Owl, and the Barn Owl.

c. There are many species of owls: the Great-Horned Owl, the Snowy Owl, and the Western Screech Owl, and the Barn Owl.

d. There are many species of owls: the Great-Horned Owl, the Snowy Owl, and the Western Screech Owl, and the Barn Owl.

22. Choose the sentence below with the correct punctuation.

a. In his most famous speech, Reverend King proclaimed: "I have a dream!"

b. In his most famous speech, Reverend King proclaimed; "I have a dream!"

c. In his most famous speech, Reverend King proclaimed. "I have a dream!"

d. In his most famous speech: Reverend King proclaimed, "I have a dream!"

23. Choose the sentence below with the correct punctuation.

a. Puzzled — Joe said, "You aren't going to pay me until ?"

b. Puzzled, Joe said, "You aren't going to pay me until ?"

c. Puzzled, Joe said, "You aren't going to pay me until —?"

d. Puzzled, Joe said, "You aren't going to pay me until, ?"

24. Choose the sentence with the correct usage.

a. Vegetables are a healthy food; eating them can make you more healthful.

b. Vegetables are a healthful food; eating them can make you more healthful.

c. Vegetables are a healthy food; eating them can make you more healthy.

d. Vegetables are a healthful food; eating them can make you more healthy.

25. Choose the sentence with the correct usage.

a. When James went into his room, he found that his clothes had been put in the closet.

b. When James went in his room, he found that his clothes had been put in the closet.

c. When James went into his room, he found that his clothes had been put into the closet.

d. When James went in his room, he found that his clothes had been put into the closet.

26. Choose the sentence with the correct usage.

a. After you lay the books on the counter, you may lay down for a nap.

b. After you lie the books on the counter, you may lay down for a nap.

c. After you lay the books on the counter, you may lie down for a nap.

d. After you lay the books on the counter, you may lay down for a nap.

27. Choose the sentence with the correct usage.

a. He did not have to loose the race; if only his shoes weren't so lose!

b. He did not have to lose the race; if only his shoes weren't so loose!

c. He did not have to loose the race; if only his shoes weren't so lose!

d. He did not have to lose the race; if only his shoes weren't so lose!

28. Choose the sentence with the correct usage.

a. The attorney did not want to prosecute the defendant; his goal was to prosecute the guilty party.

b. The attorney did not want to persecute the defendant; his goal was to persecute the guilty party.

c. The attorney did not want to prosecute the defendant; his goal was to persecute the guilty party.

d. The attorney did not want to persecute the defendant; his goal was to prosecute the guilty party.

29. Choose the sentence with the correct usage.

a. The speeches must precede the election; the election cannot proceed without hearing from the candidates.

b. The speeches must precede the election; the election cannot precede without hearing from the candidates.

c. The speeches must proceed the election; the election cannot precede without hearing from the candidates.

d. The speeches must proceed the election; the election cannot proceed without hearing from the candidates.

30. Choose the sentence with the correct usage.

a. Before a lawyer can rise an objection, he must first rise to his feet.

b. Before a lawyer can raise an objection, he must first raise to his feet.

c. Before a lawyer can raise an objection, he must first rise to his feet.

d. Before a lawyer can rise an objection, he must first raise to his feet.

Part IV – Math

1. Estimate 2009 x 108.

a. 110,000
b. 2,0000
c. 21,000
d. 210,000

2. Richard sold 12 shirts for total revenue of $336 at 8% profit. What is the purchase price of each shirt?

a. $25.76
b. $24.50
c. $23.75
d. $22.50

3. Calculate (3a + 4b) * d when A = 2, b = 4 and d = 8

a. 40
b. 150
c. 112
d. 176

4. c = 4, n = 5 and x = 3. Calculate 2cnx/2n

a. 12
b. 50
c. 8
d. 21

5. If a = 12 and b = 8, solve 6b - a + 2a

a. 12/9
b. 18
c. 16
d. 12

6. Solve √121

a. 11
b. 12
c. 21
d. None of the above

7. In a local election at polling station A, 945 voters cast their vote out of 1270 registered voters. At polling station B, 860 cast their vote out of 1050 registered voters and at station C, 1210 cast their vote out of 1440 registered voters. What was the total turnout including all three polling stations?

a. 70%
b. 74%
c. 76%
d. 80%

8. In a factory, the average salary of all employees is $125. The average salary of 10 managers is $300 and average salary of workers is $100. What is the total number of employees?

a. 30
b. 40
c. 25
d. 50

9. In a 30 minute test there are 40 problems. A student solved 28 problems in first 25 minutes. How many seconds should she give to each of the remaining problems?

a. 20 seconds
b. 23 seconds
c. 25 seconds
d. 27 seconds

10. The total expense of building a fence around a square shaped field is $2000 at a rate of $5 per meter. What is the length of one side?

a. 80 meters
b. 100 meters
c. 40 meters
d. 320 meters

11. In a class of 83 students, 72 are present. What percent of student is absent? Provide answer up to two significant digits.

a. 12
b. 13
c. 14
d. 15

12. The price of a product was increased by 45%. If the initial cost of the product was $220, what is the new cost of the product?

a. $230
b. $300
c. $290
d. $245

13. A worker's weekly salary was increased by 30%. If his new salary is $150, what was his old salary?

a. $120.00
b. $99.15
c. $109.00
d. $115.40

14. Brad has agreed to buy everyone a Coke. Each drink costs $1.89, and there are 5 friends. Estimate Brad's cost.

a. $7
b. $8
c. $10
d. $12

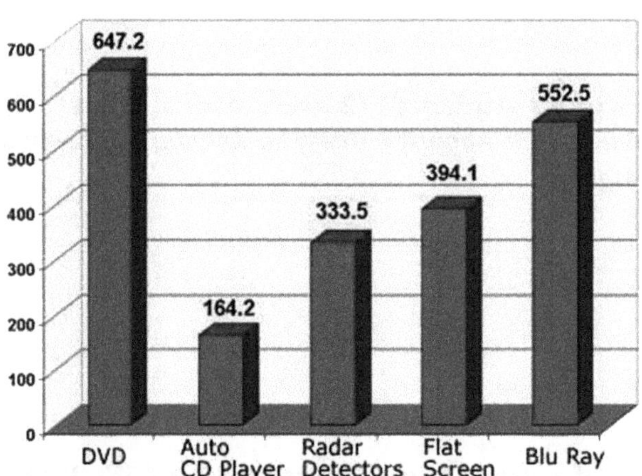

15. Consider the graph above. What is the third best-selling product?

a. Radar Detectors
b. Flat Screen TV
c. Blu Ray
d. Auto CD Players

16. Which two products are the closest in the number of sales?

a. Blu Ray and Flat Screen TV
b. Flat Screen TV and Radar Detectors
c. Radar Detectors and Auto CD Players
d. DVD players and Blu Ray

17. Great Britain has a Value Added Tax of 15%. A shop sells a camera for $545. If the VAT is included in the price, what is the actual cost of the camera?

a. $490.40
b. $473.91
c. $505.00
d. $503.15

18. The owner of a pet store decided to increase the cost of all reptiles 45%. If the initial cost of a reptile was $200, what is the new cost?

a. $230
b. $300
c. $290
d. $245

19. 5 men have to share a load weighing 10kg 550g equally among themselves. How much will each man have to carry?

a. 900 g
b. 1.5 kg
c. 3 kg
d. 2 kg 110 g

20. Peter drives 4 blocks to school and back every day. How many blocks does he drive in 5 days?

a. 20

b. 30

c. 40

d. 50

Part V - Logic

1. Consider the following sequence: 3, 5, 10, 12, 24, ... What 2 numbers should come next?

a. 48, 58

b. 26, 28

c. 48, 50

d. 26, 52

2. Consider the following sequence: 1000, 992, 984, 976, ... What 2 numbers should come next?

a. 968, 961

b. 967, 960

c. 968, 960

d. 970, 964

3. Consider the following sequence: 0.1, 0.3, 0.9, 2.7, ... What 2 numbers should come next?

a. -8.1, -24.3

b. 8.1, 24.3

c. 5.4, 10.8

d. -5.4, -10.8

4. Consider the following sequence: 32, 16, 8, 4, ... What 3 numbers should come next?

a. 2, 1, 0.5

b. 2, 0,-2

c. 0,-4,-8

d. 2, 1, 0

5. Jane spends her free time reading. She likes to read books, magazines, and even newspapers. She reads stories about adventures and fairy tales.

a. Jane likes to watch television.

b. Jane spends her free time writing stories.

c. Jane's hobby is reading.

d. Jane reads stories in school.

6. The body is made up of many bones. The skull protects the head. The ribs protect the chest. There are also small bones that protect the ears.

a. Bones are connected to the muscles.

b. Bones are present in the stomach.

c. Animals have bones.

d. Bones protect different parts of the body.

7. Trees give off oxygen. They also provide shade during sunny days. Some trees bear fruits while others are used to build houses.

a. Trees have many purposes.

b. Trees aren't important to men.

c. Birds build nests in trees.

d. Roots and trunk are parts of a tree.

8. At a liquor store, five cases of beer are stacked. There are five different types, including, Coors, Budweiser, Heineken, Molsons and Carling Lager.

1. The Coors is higher than the Carling Lager.
2. There are two cases between the Carling Lager and Heineken cases.
3. The Budweiser case is third from the top.

If the bottom case is Carling Lager, which case is on top?

a. Molsons

b. Coors

c. Heineken

d. Either Molsons or Coors

Instructions for questions 9 and 10.

1. each letter always represents the same word.
2. each word is represented by one letter.
3. the letters are not necessarily in the same order as the words.

M O R T W means

Peter loves to text Brittany

M N X T R means

Susan loves to text Mark

Q M X R T means

Andrea loves to text Susan

M Z R O Y means

Gabriel want to email Peter.

9. What letter is "Andrea?"

a. R
b. M
c. Q
d. Cannot be determined

10. What word is "Z?"

a. Text
b. Susan
c. Gabriel
d. Cannot be determined.

Scenario: You attend a break and enter and see the suspect leaving the house on Granite St., and runs north. He then turns right on San Pedro, and left on Birch. He cuts through a property on Birch and exits on Richmond. You see him taking the shortcut and continue on San Pedro, turn left on Richmond, and apprehend the suspect on Richmond as he exits the property.

11. What direction was the suspect travelling on San Pedro?

a. North
b. South
c. East
d. West

12. What direction was the suspect travelling on Birch?

a. North
b. South
c. East
d. West

13. When you turned left on Richmond, what direction were you travelling?

a. North

b. South

c. East

d. West

14. Put the statements below into the most logical sequence.

1. A woman calls the station complaining about harassment by her ex husband.
2. You receive the call from dispatch.
3. An officer takes the woman's statement.
4. You question the ex husband.
5. A judge issues a restraining order prohibiting the ex husband from contacting the woman.

a. 1, 2, 3, 4, 5

b. 1, 3, 2, 4, 5

c. 2, 3, 5, 1, 4

d. 2, 1, 3, 5, 4

15. Put the statements below into the most logical sequence.

1. You ticket one driver for dangerous driving
2. You interview both drivers separately.
3. 2 vehicles collide in the middle of an intersection
4. A vehicles runs a red light.
5. You interview pedestrians on the scene

a. 1, 2, 3, 4, 5

b. 1, 3, 2, 4, 5

c. 2, 3, 5, 1, 4

d. 4, 3, 2, 5, 1

Answer Key

Section I – Reading Comprehension

1. B
We can infer an important part of the respiratory system are the lungs. From the passage, "Molecules of oxygen and carbon dioxide are passively exchanged, by diffusion, between the gaseous external environment and the blood. This process occurs in the alveolar region of the lungs."

Therefore, a primary function for the respiratory system is the exchange of oxygen and carbon dioxide, and this process occurs in the lungs. We can therefore infer that the lungs are an important part of the respiratory system.

2. C
The process by which molecules of oxygen and carbon dioxide are passively exchanged is diffusion.

This is a definition type question. Scan the passage for references to "oxygen," "carbon dioxide," or "exchanged."

3. A
The organ that plays an important role in gas exchange in amphibians is the skin.

Scan the passage for references to "amphibians," and find the answer.

4. A
The three physiological zones of the respiratory system are Conducting, transitional, respiratory zones.

5. B
The first paragraph tells us that myths are a true account of the remote past.

The second paragraph tells us that, "myths generally take place during a primordial age, when the world was still young, before achieving its current form."

Putting these two together, we can infer that humankind

used myth to explain how the world was created.

6. A
This passage is about different types of stories. First, the passage explains myths, and then compares other types of stories to myths.

7. B
Folktales are different to myths, in that, "Unlike myths, folktales can take place at any time and any place, and the natives do not usually consider them true or sacred."

8. B
This passage describes the different categories for traditional stories. The other choices are facts from the passage, not the main idea of the passage. The main idea of a passage will always be the most general statement. For example, choice A, Myths, fables, and folktales are not the same thing, and each describes a specific type of story. This is a true statement from the passage, but not the main idea of the passage, since the passage also talks about how some cultures may classify a story as a myth and others as a folktale.

The statement, from choice B, Traditional stories can be categorized in different ways by different people, is a more general statement that describes the passage.

9. B
Choice B is the best choice, categories that group traditional stories according to certain characteristics.

Choices A and C are false and can be eliminated right away. Choice D is designed to confuse. Choice D may be true, but it is not mentioned in the passage.

10. D
The best answer is D, traditional stories themselves are a part of the larger category of folklore, which may also include costumes, gestures, and music.

All the other choices are false. Traditional stories are part of the larger category of folklore, which includes other things, not the other way around.

11. A
This passage shows there is a distinct difference between a

myth and a legend, although both are folktales.

12. D

This question tests the reader's summarization skills. The question is asking very generally about the message of the passage, and the title, "Ways Characters Communicate in Theater," is one indication of that. The other answers A, B, and C are all directly from the text, and therefore readers may be inclined to select one of them, but are too specific to encapsulate the entirety of the passage and its message.

13. B

The paragraph on soliloquies mentions "To be or not to be," and it is from the context of that paragraph that readers may understand that because "To be or not to be" is a soliloquy, Hamlet will be introspective, or thoughtful, while delivering it. It is true that actors deliver soliloquies alone, and may be "solitary" (A), but "thoughtful" (B) is more true to the overall idea of the paragraph. Readers may choose C because drama and theater can be used interchangeably and the passage mentions that soliloquies are unique to theater (and therefore drama), but this answer is not specific enough to the paragraph in question. Readers may pick up on the theme of life and death and Hamlet's true intentions and select that he is "hopeless" (D), but those themes are not discussed either by this paragraph or passage, as a close textual reading and analysis confirms.

14. C

This question tests the reader's grammatical skills. B seems logical, but parenthesis are actually considered to be a stronger break in a sentence than commas are, and along this line of thinking, actually disrupt the sentence more. A and D make comparisons between theater and film that are simply not made in the passage, and may or may not be true. This detail does clarify the statement that asides are most unique to theater by adding that it is not completely unique to theater, which may have been why the author didn't chose not to delete it and instead used parentheses to designate the detail's importance (C).

15. C

This question tests the reader's vocabulary and contextualization skills. A may or may not be true, but focuses on the wrong function of the word "give" and ignores the rest of the sentence, which is more relevant to what the passage is discussing. B and D may also be selected if the reader depends too literally on the word "give," failing to grasp the more abstract function of the word that is the focus of answer C, which also properly acknowledges the entirety of the passage and its meaning.

16. D

Tree-ferns survived the Carboniferous period. This is a fact-based question about the Carboniferous period. "Carboniferous" is an unusual word, so the fastest way to answer this question is to scan the pas-sage for the word "Carboniferous" and find the answer.

17. B

Here is the passage with the oldest to youngest trees.

The earliest trees were [1] tree ferns and horsetails, which grew in forests in the Carboniferous period. Tree ferns still survive, but the only surviving horsetails are no longer in tree form. Later, in the Triassic period, [2] conifers and ginkgos, appeared, [3] followed by flowering plants after that in the Cretaceous period.

18. D

This question tests the reader's summarization skills. The other answers A, B, and C focus on portions of the second paragraph that are too narrow and do not relate to the specific portion of text in question. The complexity of the sentence may mislead students into selecting one of these answers, but rearranging or restating the sentence will lead the reader to the correct answer. In addition, A makes an assumption that may or may not be true about the intentions of the company, B focuses on one product rather than the idea of the products, and C makes an assumption about women that may or may not be true and is not supported by the text.

19. B

This question tests reader's attention to detail. If a reader selects A, he or she may have picked up on the use of the word "debate" and assumed, very logically, that the two are at odds because they are fighting; however, this is simply not supported in the text. C also uses very specific quotes from the text, but it rearranges them and gives them false meaning. The artists want to elevate their creations above the creations of other artists, thereby showing that they are "creative" and "innovative." Similarly, D takes phrases straight from the texts and rearranges and confuses them. The artists are described as wanting to be "creative, innovative, individual people," not the women.

20. A

This question tests reader's vocabulary and summarization skills. This phrase, used by the author, may seem flippant and dismissive if readers focus on the word "whatever" and misinterpret it as a popular, colloquial terms. In this way, the answers B and C may mislead the reader to selecting one of them by including the terms "unimportant" and "stupid," respectively. D is a similar misreading, but doesn't make sense when the phrase is at the beginning of the passage and the entire passage is on media messages. A is literarily and contextually appropriate, and the reader can understand that the author would like to keep the introduction focused on the topic the passage is going to discuss.

Part II - Judgement, Recognition and Observation

Section I - Professional Judgement

1. C

One of your responsibilities is the safety, which includes yourself. In addition, a high speed chase could endanger innocent people. The best course of action is to follow the cars at a high but safe speed and update dispatch with a description of the cars and any other information you have.

2. B

A primary responsibility is to your fellow officers and this is much more important than your meeting.

3. A

The best course of action is the gather more information and then proceed from there.

4.B

Protection of life is a primary responsibility of a police officer so the best course of action is to investigate the complaint immediately. You can finish lunch later.

5. C

Handling the situation carefully and calmly is important. Stay calm and do not engage. Explain that you have found him apparently leaving the scene of a crime and would like to ask some questions

6. A

While it is important to handle the situation carefully, you have already warned him once and explained the situation. Staying calm, the best course of action is to explain that if he continues to refuse, you will have to take him to the station for questioning

7. B

The best course of action is to ask if everything is OK. No crime is being committed, and no one is being injured.

Section II - Recognition and Identification

8. A

Choice A is the same person. Choice B, while having different hair and wearing sunglasses has a wider face. Choice C and D have narrower faces.

9. A

Choice A is the same person. Choice B has a thinner face. Choice D and D have wider faces.

10. A
Choice A is the same person. Choices B and D have wider faces. Choice C has a narrower face.

Section III - Observation

11. B
Janet Benoit is wanted for child neglect.

12. C
Jeffrey Crisp is wanted for sexual assault.

13. C
The Volkswagen Phaeton is from Ontario.

14. D
Nathan Abraham is wanted for domestic assault.

15. A
The modified Chevrolet truck is from the Yukon.

Part III - Composition

1. A
Anecdote: n. A short account of an incident

2. B
Heinous: adj. shocking, terrible or wicked.

3. A
Harbinger: n. a person of thing that tells or announces the coming of someone or something

4. B
Judicious: Having, or characterized by, good judgment or sound thinking. Careful.

5. B
Ethanol: n. a colorless volatile flammable liquid C_2H_6O.

6. A
Respiratory: adj. Of, relating to, or affecting respiration or the organs of respiration.

7. B
Inherent: Naturally a part or consequence of something.

8. A
Vapid: adj. tasteless or bland.

9. C
Waif: n. homeless child or stray.

10. D
Homologous: adj. similar or identical.

11. A
Correspondence is the correct spelling.

12. C
Hemorrhage is the correct spelling.

13. B
Environment is the correct spelling.

14. D
Government is the correct spelling.

15. C
Conceive is the correct spelling.

16. A
Describe is the correct spelling.

17. B
Liquor is the correct spelling.

18. D
Successful is the correct spelling.

19. B
Hurricane is the correct spelling.

20. A
Precede is the correct spelling.

21. D
A colon informs the reader that what follows the mark proves, explains, or lists elements of what preceded the mark.

22. D
A colon informs the reader that what follows the mark proves, explains, or lists elements of what preceded the mark.

23. C
The dash is used when the speaker cannot continue.

24. D
Healthful vs. Healthy. Use 'Healthy' to describe something that is of good for your health and 'healthful' refers to habits or types.

25. A
In vs. Into. 'In' a room means inside. 'Into' refers to movement or action.

26. C
Lay vs. Lie. 'Lie' requires an object and 'lay' does not. So you can lie down, (no object. and you lay a book on the floor.

27. B
Lose vs. Loose. 'Lose' is to no longer have, or to lose a race. 'Loose' is not tied or able to move freely.

28. D
Persecute vs. Prosecute. To prosecute is to have a legal claim against someone and to persecute is to harass.

29. A
Precede vs. Proceed. To precede, is to go first or in front of. To proceed is to go forward.

30. C
Rise vs. Raise. 'Rise' does not require an object and raise does require an object. You have to 'raise' something.

Part V – Math

1. D
2009 X 108 is about 210,000. The actual number is 216,972.

2. A
The price of 12 shirts with profit is 8% = 0.92 X 336 = $309.12 The purchase price of each shirt = 309.12/12 = $25.76

3. D
Substitute the known variables, (3 x 2) + (4 x 4) x 8 =, 6 + 16 x 8, 24 x 8 = 176

4. A
2cnx = 2(4 x 5 x 3)/(2 X 5) =, 2 x 60/2 x 5 =, 120/10 = 12

5. D
Substitute with known variables, (6 x 8) – 12 + (2 x 12) =, 48 – 12 + 24, do the additions first, 48 – (12 + 24) =, 48 – 36 = 12

6. A
√121 = 11

7. D
To find the total turnout in all three polling stations, we need to proportion the number of voters to the number of all registered voters.
Number of total voters = 945 + 860 + 1210 = 3015

Number of total registered voters = 1270 + 1050 + 1440 = 3760

Percentage turnout over all three polling stations = 3015•100/3760 = 80.19%

Checking the answers, we round 80.19 to the nearest whole number: 80%

8. B
Assume the total numbers of employees is x. The total

salary of all employees will be 125x. The total salary of the managers = 10 X 300 = $3000. The number of employees = X - 10, so the total salary of employees will be 100 X (X-10). The equation becomes 100(X - 10) + 3000 = 125X. x = 40.

9. C
The number of remaining questions is 40 - 28 = 12
The time remaining is 30 - 25 = 5 minutes = 5 X 60 = 300 seconds. So the time remaining for each question is 300/12 = 25 seconds.

10. B
Total expense is $2000 and we are informed that $5 is spent per meter. Combining these two information, we know that the total length of the fence is 2000/5 = 400 meters.

The fence is built around a square shaped field. If one side of the square is "a," the perimeter of the square is "4a." Here, the perimeter is equal to 400 meters. So,

400 = 4a

100 = a → this means that one side of the square is equal to 100 meters.

11. B
If 72 students are present, then 83 - 72 = 11 students are absent. To calculate the percent, the equation will be,

11/83 = x/100
83x = 1100
x = 1100/83
x = 13.25 rounding off - 13% of the students are absent.

12. C
Initial cost was $220. new cost = 200 + 45% of 200, 45% of 200, 45/100 x 200 = 90, therefore new price is 200 + 90 = $290

13. D

Let old salary = X, therefore $150 = x + 0.30x, 150 = 1x + 0.30x, 150 = 1.30x, x = 150/1.30 = 115.4

14. C

If there are 5 friends and each drink costs $1.89, we can round up to $2 per drink and estimate the total cost at, 5 X $2 = $10.

The actual, cost is 5 X $1.89 = $9.45.

15. B

Flat Screen TVs are the third best-selling product.

16. B

The two products that are closest in the number of sales, are Flat Screen TVs and Radar Detectors.

17. B

Actual cost = X, therefore, 545 = x + 0.15x, 545 = 1x + 0.15x, 545 = 1.15x, x = 545/1.15 = 473.91

18. C

Initial cost was $220. new cost = 200 + 45% of 200, 45% of 200, 45/100 x 200 = 90, therefore new price is 200 + 90 = $290

19. D

First convert the unit of measurements to be the same. Since 1000 g = 1 kg, 10 kg = 10 x 1000 = 10,000 + 550 g = 10,550 g. Divide 10,550 by 5 = 10550/5 = 2110 = 2 kg 110 g

20. C

Each round trip will be 8 blocks, so in 5 days, he will drive 5 X 8 = 40 blocks.

Part V - Logic

1. D
The sequence is increasing by adding 2 and multiplying 2 alternatively. The next 2 terms are 24 + 2= 26 and 26 x 2 = 52.

2. C
The sequence is decreasing by 8.

3. B
The sequence is increasing by multiplying each the last term by 3. 2.7 x 3= 8.1 and 8.1 x 3 = 24.3

4. A
The sequence is decreasing by dividing the last term by 2.

5. C
The only certain thing is Jane's hobby is reading.

6. D
The only certain thing is bones protect different parts of the body.

7. A
The only certain thing is tree have many purposes.

8. C
Given information is that Carling Lager is on the bottom, and #3 says Budweiser is 3rd from the top. #2 says there are two cases between the Carling Lager and Heineken cases, so the Heineken case must be in position 2.

1.
2. Heineken case
3. Budweiser case
4.
5. Carling Lager case

Molsons and Coors are still unknown. #1 says the Coors case is higher than the Carling Lager case, but since we know the Carling Lager case is on the bottom, that doesn't help. Therefore, we cannot determine the positions of the Molsons or Coors cases.

9. C

"Andrea" is only in sentence 3. Since and all three sentences only differ in the names, the corresponding letters found in all three, M R and T must be "loves to text."

"Susan" must correspond to "X," as they both appear in sentences 2 and 3. To find "Andrea," which only appears in sentence 3, look for the only other letter in that sentence, which is Q.

10. D

"M" and "R" appear in all four sentences, so they must be "loves" and "to" which also appear in all four.
The letters "Z" and "Y" only appear in sentence #4. The other difference between sentence #4 are the words "email" and "Gabriel," but we cannot determine which.

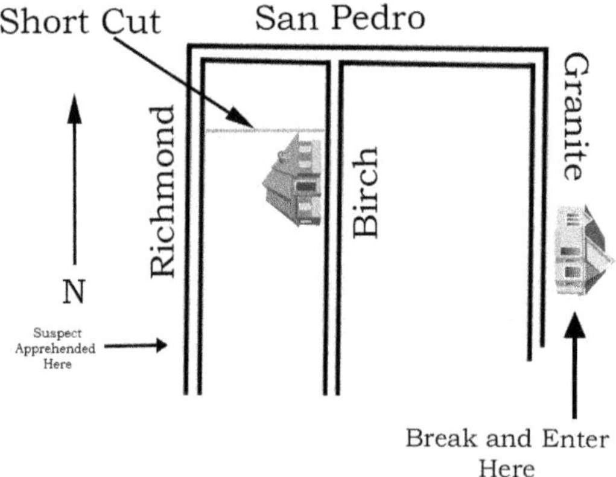

11. D

The suspect was travelling west on San Pedro.

12. B
The suspect was travelling south on Birch.

13. B
You were travelling south when you turned left on Richmond.

14. B
1, 3, 2, 4, 5 is the correct sequence.

1. A woman calls the station complaining about harassment by her ex husband.
3. An officer takes the woman's statement.
2. You receive the call from dispatch.
4. You question the ex husband.
5. A judge issues a restraining order prohibiting the ex husband from contacting the woman.

15. D
4, 3, 2, 5, 1 is the correct sequence.

4. A vehicles runs a red light.
3. 2 vehicles collide in the middle of an intersection
2. You interview both drivers separately.
5. You interview pedestrians on the scene
1. You ticket one driver for dangerous driving

Conclusion

CONGRATULATIONS! You have made it this far because you have applied yourself diligently to practicing for the exam and no doubt improved your potential score considerably! Getting into a good school is a huge step in a journey that might be challenging at times but will be many times more rewarding and fulfilling. That is why being prepared is so important.

Good Luck!

FREE Ebook Version

Go to http://tinyurl.com/pw7zzvu

Register for Free Updates and More Practice Test Questions

Register your purchase at

www.test-preparation.ca/register.html for fast and convenient access to updates, errata, free test tips and more practice test questions.

Endnotes

Reading Comprehension passages where noted below are used under the Creative Commons Attribution-ShareAlike 3.0 License

http://en.wikipedia.org/wiki/Wikipedia:Text_of_Creative_Commons_Attribution-ShareAlike_3.0_Unported_License

[1] Immune System. In Wikipedia. Retrieved November 12, 2010 from, en.wikipedia.org/wiki/Immune_system.

[2] White Blood Cell. In Wikipedia. Retrieved November 12, 2010 from en.wikipedia.org/wiki/White_blood_cell.

[3] Infectious disease. In Wikipedia. Retrieved November 12, 2010 from http://en.wikipedia.org/wiki/Infectious_disease.

[4] Virus. In Wikipedia. Retrieved November 12, 2010 from en.wikipedia.org/wiki/Virus.

[5] Thunderstorm. In Wikipedia. Retrieved November 12, 2010 from en.wikipedia.org/wiki/Thunderstorm.

[6] Meteorology. In Wikipedia. Retrieved November 12, 2010 from en.wikipedia.org/wiki/Outline_of_meteorology.

[7] Cloud. In Wikipedia. Retrieved November 12, 2010 from http://en.wikipedia.org/wiki/Clouds.

[8] U.S. Navy Seal. In Wikipedia. Retrieved November 12, 2010 from en.wikipedia.org/wiki/United_States_Navy_SEALs.

[9] Respiratory System. In Wikipedia. Retrieved November 12, 2010 from en.wikipedia.org/wiki/Respiratory_system.

[10] Mythology. In Wikipedia. Retrieved November 12, 2010 from en.wikipedia.org/wiki/Mythology.

[11] Tree. In Wikipedia. Retrieved November 12, 2010 from en.wikipedia.org/wiki/Tree.

[12] Insect. In Wikipedia. Retrieved November 12, 2010 from en.wikipedia.org/wiki/Insect.

CPSIA information can be obtained
at www.ICGtesting.com
Printed in the USA
LVHW01s0350240917
549693LV00001B/5/P